SHOPIFY
SECRETS

Shopify
Secrets

Introduction to this Book

Part One: Introduction to ecommerce

Chapters

Part Two: Setting up Shopify

Part Three: Making your Shopify store a success.

Conclusion to this Book

Introduction

Welcome to Shopify Secrets! Having your own ecommerce website is one of the most rewarding and fulfilling things that you can do in your life. Knowing that you have the potential for unlimited income and that it all rests on how hard you work is very liberating and motivating. While having an online store is something that many people dream about, few actually follow through and build one, so you are in a unique class of individuals. Of course, creating a store has never been easier either, thanks to Shopify. In fact, setting up and launching an ecommerce website is as simple as painless as creating a Wordpress or Blogger blog these days thanks to ecommerce platforms like Shopify.

What You Need to Start Your Own Ecommerce Website

There are some initial things that you should be bringing to the table if you plan to start your own ecommerce website, before you start configuring your store or even deciding what sort of products you are going to sell. You should ask yourself if you have or are willing to cultivate the items on the list below to give yourself the best chance possible of having success at selling online. Here are a few things to consider if you are thinking of getting into the business.

- Are you able to devote the time involved into making your store successful? That may include several hours per week that you spend setting up your ecommerce website while still having to work a full-time job or assume your regular responsibilities. Even if you are able to be successful and work your store full-time you will have to spend time each week on order fulfillment, shipping, updating your store, communicating with customers and following the industry of products that you are selling.

- Do you have the ability to invest in your store while still meeting your financial responsibilities and possibly compromising the lifestyle that you are used to in order to have money to spend on setting up your store? Even if you take out a loan to start your store you are still assuming financial risk and you need to make sure that you are prepared financially.

- Can you work on your store for a year or more without seeing any sort of profit? The Small Business Administration estimates that the average small business won't see a profit until the second or third year in business.

- Will you be able to keep yourself motivated even if you feel as if you aren't having any success at running your store? You may end up having to work for a long period of time before you see any sort of success and most people would give up before they reached the point where things turned around for them. Are you able to make yourself accomplish the work that needs to be done daily, as well as live your regular life, including working at another job, all with what seems like to reward at any time in the near future.

- Are you prepared to accept potential defeat? You might put in the work, live simply or take out a loan to have money to invest in your business, purchase a great deal of inventory and do countless other things to make your website a success only to realize that it is never going to work the way that you have it currently set up. The competition is fierce and it not only takes skill and perseverance to run a successful e-store, it also takes luck. It is possible that you'll never be able to get your business off of the ground and you have to be willing to take that risk.

Why You Should Start an Ecommerce Website

Even though it might sound like starting an ecommerce website is best left to people with a great deal of time on their hands and plenty of money to invest, there are some great reasons to take on the challenge. Yes, it is a difficult job, but there are also benefits that make up for the difficulty of the process. Here are some of the more positive aspects and results of starting your own ecommerce store.

- You get to be your own boss. That means that you have no one telling you what to do, and that any successes (or failures) are yours and yours alone. Many people dream of being their own boss and dislike their current job or supervisor, but few actually get the opportunity to do so. You'll definitely be accomplishing something that lots of people dream about.

- You can work from home. That's right; you don't have to go into the office. You don't have to leave your house at all. You can skip the shower if you want. You can work barefoot, in your underwear or however else you choose (with the shades down of course). Besides the comfort factor, you also have the ability to work whatever hours you choose and take time off whenever you want. If you decide you want to work for ten days and then take five off, no one will stop you. Of course, if you are shipping merchandise yourself, you might be limited by the needs of your customers but you'll still have a great deal of freedom.

- You have the potential to make an unlimited amount of money. You know that in your regular job, no matter how hard you work, the most that you can look forward to is a series of raises. Even if you had the best luck in the world and worked harder than anyone else, you aren't going to get rich from your paychecks. But with an e-store, the harder you work and the luckier you get, the more money you'll make. Becoming a millionaire is within the realm of possibility when you are business for yourself.

- You'll be prepared for the future. The fact is: brick-and-mortar stores are on their way out. If the technology is created to ship something and have it arrive at the customer's home or business within hours, such as with Amazon's drone shipping program or through the use of 3-D printers, brick-and-mortar stores will have no advantages and many disadvantages. Right now, the only thing they have going for them is that you get the item when you buy it. In the future, it is likely that any benefits to shopping in person will be outweighed by the benefits of online shopping and you will be right there, already prepared to fulfill the online shopping in your niche.

- You get numerous advantages over starting a retail store. There are many advantages that ecommerce has over the brick-and-mortar retail store for business owners, perhaps even more benefits than for customers. For example: you get to stay open 24 hours a day, 365 days a year. Can you imagine how much it would cost to run a physical retail store 24 hours? Also, you don't have to pay rent, you don't have to pay utilities and start-up costs are massively reduced.

Why You Should Start a Shopify Store

While there are some enormous benefits to starting an ecommerce website, there may be even more benefits to doing it with the Shopify platform. In fact, many of the risks and the potential problems mentioned in this introduction that come with having your own e-store are minimized or eliminated thanks to the Shopify platform. Whether or not you start an ecommerce business is up to you, but if you decide you are going to, you definitely need to do it using the Shopify platform. Here are just a few reasons.

1. Your store design costs normally would be thousands of dollars, for getting a website designer that not only has the skills to create a great looking website, but also to program all of the ecommerce functions you need including security. But with Shopify, there is no huge investment of thousands of dollars. You just pay one of four tiers of pricing and you get the perfect ecommerce website.

2. You get the benefit of the entire Shopify team. You aren't just getting a website template with Shopify, you are getting a ready-made store that has already had all of the bugs worked out and has been re-designed and re-worked so that it functions perfectly and has just about every feature that you could possibly want.

3. The platform is so intuitive that you can start building your store right after logging in. You might have to look at the help pages to use some of the more advanced features but for adding products and customizing design as well as other basics, you can start doing it right away with almost no learning curve.

4. You have some incredible security. By law, an ecommerce website has to take certain steps to protect a customer's financial information, but you don't just get sufficient security with Shopify, you get some of the most highly rated security features of any ecommerce platform on the market today. You don't have to worry about programming security protocols or making sure that your site is

protected on all sides from thieves who want your customer's credit card numbers. Shopify does all the work for you.

5. Shopify is designed to help you reach your SEO potential. If you were to pay a designer for a custom ecommerce site you would spend thousands of dollars or perhaps even tens of thousands of dollars and you wouldn't get the features that you get with Shopify. One of those features is their search engine optimization. With Shopify, your e-store has the best chance possible to rank high in the search engines and bring you lots of organic traffic.

6. You get analytics that tell you exactly what is going on. With Shopify, you can see exactly where your customers are coming from, what keywords they are using to reach your site and where they go once they get there, not to mention how long they stay. All of this information has one primary purpose – to allow you to tweak your Shopify site and your marketing and promotion efforts to get as many people coming to your site as possible and then getting them to stay there once they arrive. You still have to offer great products, but Shopify helps you market your site much more effectively and gets customers to show up, which is half the battle when it comes to ecommerce.

7. Your site is already optimized for mobile and will continue to be optimized in the future. With Shopify, you get a responsive website that will work with any mobile device and as this quickly becomes the primary way that people shop, your ecommerce website is only going to get better, as the engineers behind the platform ensure that you always keep up with the technology.

8. You get hosting with your site. Shopify has an advantage that many ecommerce platforms do not share – your site is hosted by them, and your payment gateway and other shopping cart features are already taken care of. Not only does this save you money since you don't have to pay for hosting, you also will always have enough bandwidth to support your traffic and of course, you get security with the hosting that is unrivaled.

9. Shopify is extremely reliable. Shopify didn't get to their spot as the number one ecommerce platform by accident. They are so popular and so widely used because of how reliable the platform is. When your store begins to get more traffic, you will lose money for every second or minute that your site id own. Using Shopify minimizes the chances of this as much as possible.

10. Shopify has numerous apps created for your use. The Shopify app store has some talented designers creating programs that you can use to make your ecommerce store even better. You can customize the appearance of your site and do a great deal with Shopify but with the app store you can create an unstoppable force in the world of ecommerce.

What this Book is about

This book is intended to explain everything that you need to know about the Shopify platform, including why to use it, how to use it and what sort of products and services the platform is appropriate for. The main purpose of the book is to take you through the process of deciding whether or not to use the program, then a step-by-step guide to choosing your products and setting up your Shopify store. There are three sections to this eBook:

Part One: Introduction to Ecommerce

This section is an introduction to the world of ecommerce in general and includes information on how to decide what products to fill your store with, how to evaluate the competition that your store is likely to face, how to differentiate between the different products that are out there, how to identify your ideal consumer and how to become unique and an indispensible ecommerce website that is known for having expertise in a specific niche. You will understand the various aspects of the ecommerce industry including how to position yourself as an expert in your field and understand laws and regulations that pertain to you.

Part Two: Setting up Shopify

The second part of this book is all about the Shopify platform. This section of the eBook will show you exactly how to set up your Shopify site, including choosing a Shopify package that will work best for you, creating and customizing your Shopify store. These chapters will teach you everything that you need to know about setting up payment gateways, calculating sales tax and saving for income tax, offering shipping options and how to launch your ecommerce website most effectively.

Part Three: Making Your Shopify Store a Success

The final part of this eBook will deal with the extras that you can add on to your Shopify site as well as ways that you can market your website without spending money doing so. You'll learn how to optimize your site for search engines, how to use social media to market your site and still retain your followers as well as taking advantage of time-sensitive factors like trends when they happen so that you can make as much money as possible and allow your ecommerce website to reach its full potential. From extra features to social media, this section is all about making your ecommerce site as good as it can possibly be.

Part One: Introduction to Ecommerce

Chapter One
Choosing Products That Are Right for Your Store

When it comes to selling online, particularly with a platform like Shopify, you want to choose products that work well with the platform, as well as products the work well for your particular store. Luckily, you can sell just about anything using Shopify and you'll see that people have created stores with almost every product imaginable. But what about choosing products that are right for you? That's a little more complicated and you're going to have to ask yourself some thoughtful questions to figure out what it is that you want to sell in your Shopify store.

Choosing Your Products: Go With What You Know

The first thing that you should understand is that while you don't need to be an expert on whatever products or services that you are selling, you at least need to be familiar enough with them to be able to answer a customer's questions or to know where to go to find the answers when you don't know it yourself. So, the best place to start is to decide what you are passionate about. If you are an avid action figure collector perhaps toys is your particular niche. If you are into sewing and knitting, then those particular hobbies might be where your production selection should come from.

Identify a Problem & Solve it

Second, we want to identify a need. Everyone has problems that they want solved by a product. When they find that product, they are willing to fork over cash for it. A good example is the weight loss industry. Experts have been saying for decades now that there is no "magic pill" for weight loss. In fact, there is nothing except hard work that promotes weight loss – less calories in and more calories burned. But still, there are thousands of "magic pill" weight loss products on the market, cluttering up the television late at night and advertised in every magazine and newspaper in the country.

Obviously, those people are still in business because people are willing to pay for what they want, and what they want is a magic weight loss solution that will allow them to skip the dieting and exercise. Unfortunately, those products don't work. Hopefully, you will find a need or a problem that begs to be solved and actually provide a product that will solve that problem. If you do, you'll be ahead of more than three-quarters of the ecommerce entrepreneurs out there, because many people don't consider what problems need to be solved when they start to sell, nor do they ensure that they have chosen a product that will solve that problem effectively. Many new sellers simply jump in with both feet.

Think About it From a Consumer Standpoint

Have you ever purchased something? Of course you have. In fact, it is certain that you have purchased many things during your lifetime. You have been a consumer, and so you have the ability to look at your products and your store from a consumer point-of-view. Imagine that you were trying to solve the problem from the last section yourself. What kind of things would you be looking for? Would you be looking for a real, physical product or would a service help you better? What kind of features would you want that product to have? What other things would you be willing to buy as accessories to that product or service?

These questions are how you look at your product from a consumer point-of-view. It is easy to get lost in the business owner point-of-view, where you think that if you build your store, they will come, even if you aren't sure who "they" are or what they are looking for. You can not only solve your customer's problems much more effectively when you are able to see things from their perspective, you are also able to cash in on extras, like the aforementioned accessories. When you think you have the products that you want to sell, spend some time carefully considering them as a customer before you commit to putting them into your store.

Your Brand as a Marketing Tool

Okay, so you might not have a brand built up yet, but it is important to evaluate whether or not you are going to be able to make your brand have staying power in the niche that you have decided upon. This is an almost impossible decision to make until you know more about how your business is going to go. Your brand could be the best way that you could have possibly marketed yourself or it could lead to your downfall if you don't change it. But as mentioned, it is impossible to predict. As an example, a successful attorney was unfortunately enough to have the last name "Crooks." When he went live with an ad campaign that was branded "Trust Crooks" everyone thought it would backfire, but in fact, it turned out to be successful for him.

Even if you can't predict exactly how your brand and marketing is going to fare when it actually gets in front of consumers, there are a few things that you can do to ensure that you have the best chance possible to make it a success. Here are some things to keep in mind when building your store brand.

1. The Logo: You don't want to go with a logo that someone from Fiverr made for you, or even one of those "Make-it-yourself" logo services. You definitely don't want to design it yourself until you actually are a graphic designer. Instead, spend some money and get a real, professional logo created. If you can't afford the outlay, try to make a trade with a graphic designer.

2. Something Completely Unique: Brands that become successful do so because they offer something that no one else offers and then they market the heck out of that feature. For example: Tom's Shoes is a for-profit shoe company that sells their canvas kicks for probably more than you think they're worth, but they

donate a pair of shoes to a child in need in a third-world country with every purchase, so people buy from them in droves. Remember the old Domino's Pizza ads? "Thirty minutes or it's free!" They've had to stop guaranteeing that particular time frame since driver's were getting into car accidents, but the principle stands.

3. Being Consistent: This is a biggie. Think about readers and successful authors. The readers that flock to those authors in droves do so because the writer delivers one great story after another, consistently. In fact, what readers want when they finish a great book by an author is another book just like it. It can work the same for your business. If you solve a problem for them in a particular niche and provide a quality product, they will expect you to be able to solve a similar problem in the future and with the same level of quality as the first.

So, choosing products is more than just selling something you like. You want products that you know a lot about, enjoy working with and can build a brand around. Do that and your Shopify site will be successful.

Chapter Two
Determining Your Market Size

Once you have decided what kind of products you are going to sell, you next need to determine how big the market is for those products. There are a number of mistakes that some new entrepreneurs make when setting up their store for the first time. We'll go over a few of those in a moment. If you can avoid the mistakes, then you have a much better chance of being successful. Determining market size definitely is one of the most important things that you can do before setting up your store, but do keep mind that even if you determine that the market is too small for the product that you have chosen, you might still be able to sell it.

That's one of the first mistakes that people make when they are determining their market size. They stubbornly stick to one product because it is their passion and that's why they got into the business in the first place. There's nothing wrong with that, except that if you want to be successful, you are going to have to do more than sell a product that almost no one wants. So, how do you do you appeal to a wider customer base while still selling something that you are familiar with or knowledgeable about. There are actually two ways that this can be accomplished.

Method One: Expand Your Product Line

So, you want to sell bandanas or 'do rags that feature horses. This is a great product – for someone who wants to wear a bandana that features horses. But there aren't many people looking for that particular product. In fact, you might be hard-pressed to sell a single bandanna. But there is definitely a market for 'do rags and bandannas. The problem is, there is too much competition in this wider market, which is why you went with the niche – that and your unparalleled expertise on horse prints and patterns of course. But what if you decided to sell bandannas that featured all kinds of animal, pop culture and photo print designs. You suddenly have opened yourself up to a huge market of bandanna and 'do rag wearing customers.

Method Two: Learn Something New

Okay, so maybe your niche product only appeals to a very specific niche and there isn't anything you can do to expand it. You don't want to stick with that niche on a potentially huge ecommerce site like your Shopify site. Instead, you want to learn something new. Simply move on to a new niche and if you don't know anything about it, then you can learn before you open your store. Of course, you can always find something that is related to your original niche idea so that you can at least incorporate the products that you had in mind at some later date when you have already established a name for yourself with the new niche.

Don't be Afraid to Choose a Large Market

Another mistake that budding entrepreneurs make when they are first setting up their store is to balk at competing in a large market. If you are looking at your market and feeling fearful that you will get lost in the shuffle, take heart. There are actually several things that you can do to distinguish yourself in a large market to make sure that you can compete with the big guys. We'll go over those strategies in a later chapter.

How to Determine the Size of a Market

So, how do you determine the size of a market for a product that you are considering selling? The first step is to check out the market research that has already been done for you. There is no reason not to take advantage of information that is provided by the government, not-for-profit organizations or even companies that have released the information. To determine the size of the market you'll research your industry with the Small Business Administration or through FedStats.gov. There are also organizations devoted to each industry that will have more accurate numbers. Checking out these numbers is the first step in determining market size, but not the last one, because you are likely competing in a niche market within that consumer segment.

Determine Your Niche Market

If you are competing in a niche market then you are going to want to narrow down the market segment that you figured out by researching the industry into a much smaller number, because you aren't likely to find specific numbers on your particular niche unless it is incredibly broad. For example, if you are selling bandanas, you wouldn't be able to get numbers on how many people buy bandanas and 'do rags but you might be able to get specific numbers on how many people in the country are buying health and beauty products – hint: it's almost all of them. That's unfortunately how the numbers are structured. Luckily there are some solid ways to narrow down your market and be fairly accurate.

Demographics

We're going to go into demographics in detail in the next chapter. But we'll have to skip ahead just a little to make a point here. In order to narrow down your niche market, you're going to have to read chapter three and follow the instructions there, because you can't have one without the other. Your ideal customer will determine what demographics you look at, and that will determine what your market size is going to be. As for the demographics that make up your ideal customers, that will be up to you based upon your research.

Estimating Market Size by Competition

Another way that you can estimate the market size of the niche that you are going to be working in is by looking at the competition. For example: if you were to go to Amazon and look at their book selection under the 'Arts & Photography' category, you will notice that while 'Architecture' has more than 10,000 books in that subcategory, the subcategory 'Dance' only has about 1000. That means that you can safely assume that the dance book niche is about 10% of the size of the architecture book niche. You don't have to use Amazon for this method, but if you can, it is usually pretty accurate.

If you don't want to use Amazon's listings, or your particular niche isn't represented there, you can use the search engines with the same effect. For example: suppose that you were selling bandannas with famous movie stars on them. If you were to type in 'bandanas' you could check out the competition that comes up and see how many of them (if any) are offering movie star bandanas.

Even better, if you have a Google account, you can use the Adwords Keyword Planner to type in phrases that will allow you to see just how many people search monthly for a particular keyword phrase. For example, you might type in 'Tiger print bandanas' and see that more than 1000 people every month search for that particular item. That means that if you sold tiger print bandanas and you could get your website in front of those people, you'd make some sales.

So, determining your market size isn't that difficult. But it's not all that accurate either, unless you willing to spend tens of millions on market research.

Chapter Three
Identifying Your Target Customer

The next thing that you're going to have to do is identify the customer that you are trying to connect with. You've got a product niche all picked out and you've determined that the market size is sufficient to allow you to make money in said niche, but what about the actual person that is going to buy that product? You can't market to a faceless crowd. You need to know who is most likely to buy your product or use your service so that you can tailor your marketing specifically for them and entice them to buy from you. Understanding your ideal customer starts with a basic understanding of how demographics work.

Demographics: How to Know Which Group to Market to

Some companies couldn't live without demographic data. That is the only way that they can make decisions, create marketing strategies and plan elaborate ad campaigns. To be fair, we are talking about tens or even hundreds of millions of dollars invested in some cases so it is no wonder that they evaluate their marketing plan carefully before they implement it. But for the average ecommerce website that specializes in a particularly niche, market data isn't a necessity. It is however, extremely useful. But to understand the data, you first have to understand how the groups are divided.

Demographic Attributes

To understand what sort of factors make up your target consumer, you need to understand what sort of categories that the experts divide people into. Here are just some of those categories.

- Men
- Women
- Men & Women 18-24
- Men & Women 35 to 34
- Men & Women 35 to 54
- Men & Women Age 55 and Over
- Level of education
- Size of the Household
- Ethnicity
- Race
- Income
- Occupation

So, you can see that identifying the ideal customer is a little more complicated than it looks on the surface and what goes into actually getting that information is even more difficult to understand. There are of course, some products that demographics are easy for. For example: if you were marketing tampons, you'd want to market them exclusively to women between the ages of puberty and menopause. If you were marketing cologne on the other hand, you might market the same basic age groups for men on the other side.

However, other information is harder to come by. When a company wants to know who is more apt to buy their product, they have several ways to get the information. The most common one is paying for surveys. You might even have worked at one of these survey centers if you are part of Generation Y. Now, they are pretty much obsolete as the internet has made it incredibly easy to collect data. Companies spend millions tracking consumers as they shop, as they window shop and as they search for things that they'd rather not have Wal-Mart know about. Of course, this data is compiled and separated, and usually tells companies with a great deal of accuracy what kind of person is looking for the products that they sell.

Unfortunately, this method doesn't usually work for the average consumer, particularly not one just starting their own Shopify store. So, your method will have to be a little different. Even if you have no clue whatsoever who will be buying your products right now, there are some ways that you can identify your target consumer. Here are some tips.

How Small Businesses & Ecommerce Sites Can Identify Their Target Market

The first thing that we're going to do is refer back to the beginning of this book. Remember the problem that you are solving? Well, that's the first step to identifying your target customer. What kind of person would be having the kind of problem that your product or service solves? From there you can begin to narrow things down a little bit. Is that person more likely to be male or female? What age range is this person apt to be in? Questions like these can help you begin to define your ideal audience.

Create a Picture of the Customer(s) in Your Head

Remember, your ideal customer doesn't have to be limited to just one person. You can create an archetype that encompasses several different age ranges, genders or income brackets. The important thing is that you create a picture of these customers in your head – in other words that you actually consider these customers to be real people and not just faceless cardboard cutouts in front of computer screens. Make an actual list of the customers you think that your product is right for, and divide them up by demographics like gender, age group and location.

See the Value in Your Product or Service

If you are having trouble narrowing down just what your ideal customer is going to be then you might need to ask yourself some defining questions to identify who would consider your product or service to be valuable. Here are some questions that you can use to paint a picture if you had trouble with this in the previous step.

1. What is the problem again and what type of person is likely to suffer the most from it?
2. If the customer does not deal with this problem using your product or service, what will the result be? What will happen if they fail to act?

Understand Your Market

Obviously, you are going to be a niche provider. Every small ecommerce company is a niche provider these days. The world of internet marketing and ecommerce is one that requires a niche in order to compete, and the more specialized a niche the better (assuming there is a market for it). Identifying your ideal customer requires that you understand your market intimately. Can you imagine if Roy Raymond had never been married or tried to buy his wife lingerie? Would Victoria's Secret have been as successful as it is? Raymond was able to compete in the industry and grow his company to be the world's largest intimate clothing retailer.

Up until that point, no one had thought of marketing lingerie to men. It was inconceivable. After all, men didn't wear lingerie. But Raymond discovered that the ideal customer was just like him and obviously, since he knew himself intimately, it was quite easy for him to begin marketing to his ideal customer. He created the perfect situation for himself to be successful – identifying who was most likely to buy his products and then laser targeting his marketing efforts towards them. That's not to say that Victoria's Secret didn't target women as well – they did – but at the time marketing lingerie to men was revolutionary – and it made Roy Raymond rich.

Understand Your Customer's Options

The previous example is also a demonstration of this principle. What options does the ideal customer have? This will help you decide who the ideal customer is, because you want them to have no option other than yourself. That's why the aforementioned Victoria's Secret was able to become the number one lingerie retailer in America. Men had no other option when it came to buying lingerie, except visiting the same stores that they had become embarrassed in and likely were unable to complete their purchases.

Chapter Four
Evaluating the Competition

Unless you truly are in the equine bandanna niche, you are going to have competition and probably a lot of it. But it's not as scary as it sounds. In fact, most of the people out there are floundering in their new ecommerce business just like you are, and even the ones who have their doo-doo together you can learn something from. So, just because there are others competing in your same niche, don't think that you aren't going to be able to compete. Instead, look at it as a challenge and more importantly, think of something unique that you can do or provide that would make people want to come and shop with you.

How to Know Who the Competition is

If you want to evaluate the competition, you first need to know who that competition is. If you sell tennis shoes, you can bet that the athletic stores, department stores, smaller online shoe sellers and discount websites will all be your competition. Even if you don't sell shoes, you can pretty much count on Amazon competing with you on just about every real-world product you can think of. There are only a few pies that they haven't gotten their fingers in yet, and it is only a matter of time.

But what if you sell something that isn't so easy to define the competition for? Well, let's go back to the trusty bandana, aka 'do rag. Some people also call them scarves and both men and women wear them, usually on their head. A quick search in Google will show you that some of the top competitors for 'bandana' are some pretty well-known real-world stores like Hobby Lobby and Michaels. Of course, Amazon is at the top of the search results for this particular term. They usually are.

Luckily, you aren't trying to compete for bandanas. You're going to make a list of keywords that people use when they are searching for a particular type of bandana. To learn what people are typing in, you have two tried-and-true methods. The first is the Google Auto-Complete method.

Using Google Instant to Identify Your Products & Competitors

If you have Google instant search (also known as auto-complete) turned on then you'll be able to see suggestions as you type. It's like Google is convinced that you don't know what you're trying to type into the search field. Even so, it makes a great way for you to see what people are looking for, and afterward, to see what companies are providing those products.

So, if you were to use Google Instant Search when it came to bandanas, you might begin by typing in the word 'bandana.' Unfortunately, this example doesn't lend itself well to demonstration because most of the descriptive terms that would narrow down your bandana selection appear before the word, not after. However, you can still use Google Instant to come up with some ideas by typing in a descriptive phrase and the word 'bandana' and then seeing what else comes up. For instance, if you were to type 'tiger stripe bandana' into Google Instant, you might notice that 'camo bandana' comes up a lot.

Once you have determined some of the keywords that describe products similar to those that you're going to be selling, your next step is to see who is selling under those keywords. It is important to distinguish that while you can use this method to come up with keywords for your own site or even for you to come up with a particular niche product to sell, the goal here is simply to see what kind of competitors are in the field by using related keywords. Ideally, you aren't going to find very many (read: hopefully none) competitors that are selling exactly what you are, but if you look at some of the related products you'll be able to develop a picture of the competition.

Using the Google Keyword Planner to Determine Competitors

If you're in an ecommerce business you are going to have competitors that are trying to rank for keywords just like you are. It is likely that they developed their strategy using the Google Keywords Planner. Therefore, if you can use it to get some of the more popular search terms related to your particular niche, you'll be able to see what kind of competition is out there. All you have to do is type in something related to your keyword and then see what kind of keywords come up. You want to use the "Get Keyword Ideas" part of the planner and if you aren't familiar with how to use the tool, Google offers a comprehensive tutorial section.

Checking Out the Competition

In either of these cases, you are going to end up with search results of companies that sell the same thing that you do. What you want to look for are actual ecommerce stores that sell products. If you come across a blog that happens to be talking about bandanas (or whatever your product is) and has Amazon affiliate items available in the sidebar, ignore it. You only want to evaluate ecommerce websites that are at least as serious as your Shopify site.

Make a list of the competitors that pop up again and again when you try out various related keywords. Those companies – even if they don't sell the exact same thing you do – are going to be who you are competing against – at least for the most popular keywords. You might rank at the top of a search for a particular niche search (equine design bandanas anyone?) but that doesn't mean you are going to get traffic. You want to find out who is competing against you for keywords that will actually bring you traffic.

Evaluating That Competition

The last thing that you are going to do is decide how much of a threat this competition actually is to you. This is actually one of the easier things to do with the internet, because internet marketing is such a booming business that there are literally hundreds of thousands of marketing tools that will let you take a peek at what the other guys are doing.

You might remember that a site's pagerank used to be a big deal. Now, it isn't necessarily an indicator of how strong a site is (although you can't discount it completely) and backlinks are the same way. You used to be able to tell exactly how you would be able to outrank a site by targeting the same keywords and getting more backlinks than they had.

Now, Google has changed their algorithm drastically. But you can still evaluate a company's strength by looking at some of the other factors that exist. For example: Google loves it when you have content on your website – and the more high quality content, the better. If you have a blog that published quality articles regularly, you'll be poised to be regarded as an expert in that particular field. The world of SEO and evaluating the strength of a website is an industry in itself, but if you learn what makes a website strong, you can make your site even stronger and rise above the competition.

Chapter Five
Making Yourself Unique Among Your Competitors

So, you have learned how to identify your product, how to extrapolate a picture of your ideal customer archetypes and how to determine how strong the competition is in the particular niche you are trying to compete in. But how do you give yourself an advantage over all of those other people competing for the dollars being spent in your niche? That's actually not as complicated as you might think and it's not that difficult either. Plus, you'd be surprised how many ecommerce businesses out there actually fail to take this one important step.

Instead, these companies create "cookie cutter" or "clone" businesses that look like a pale imitation of whatever site they are trying to emulate. There's nothing wrong with trying to be successful like your favorite store, but there is something wrong with creating a website that looks almost exactly the same and sells the same products. You don't want to be a clone of a website that is selling; you want to be unique in the midst of these successful websites which will also make you successful. In other words, don't be a follower. Make your business into a trendsetting – a leader in the field and don't be afraid to take some chances. If you want to make your business stand out among the competition here are some ways to do exactly that.

Go Above & Beyond

If you want to make your company stand out among all of the others out there then you need to work harder than they are willing to work and that means giving more to your customers than other companies are willing to give. Whether that means manning your Twitter until the wee hours of the morning to do customer support, or paying for options that make the customer experience better, you'll find that companies that are willing to go the extra mile for their customers will end up with loyal buyers who will rarely go elsewhere, even if someone else has a better price. Whatever you do, don't be ordinary. There are many 'average' companies out there that have nothing to make them stand out above the rest; be a mediocre company and you'll get mediocre sales.

Create a Winning Brand

If you want staying power in a competitive market, you need to make your brand stand out above all else. You want to make sure that you are the company that someone thinks about when they think about a product that you sell. Think about some of the most successful companies in the world for various products and services. Who do you think of when you think of fried chicken? Church's? KFC? What about when you think of tools and hardware? ACE is probably pretty high on your list. That's because these companies have created a winning brand. They have used advertising, marketing and plain old hard work to make themselves one of the top companies in the nation for that niche.

Make Your Marketing Memorable

You've heard of viral videos? Well, that's one of the most effective ways that people make their marketing memorable. Superbowl commercials are another way. The plan here is to create a marketing effort that is so successful at sticking in people's minds that they think of your brand later on, hopefully when they are in a position to buy a product or service that you offer. You don't necessarily have to create a viral video to make your marketing memorable (although if you can pull it off, that's an extremely effective method of getting your name out there) but you do need to make sure that every marketing effort you make is as memorable as you can design it.

Create a Compelling Blog

You've probably heard that a blog is one of the best ways to market your business. That is true for several reasons. First, the more content you have on your website, and particularly if you are publishing fresh content each week, the more authoritative your site becomes. Second, with each blog post that you create you target more keywords and if you can find a way to funnel the traffic that comes in via your blog posts over to your sales page, you will be turning those blog posts into cold, hard cash.

However, creating a blog isn't enough. You need to create a blog that people actually want to read. Publishing a boring blog post might get you some traffic to your blog with the keywords that you create, but it isn't going to make people stick around and read that blog post, nor is it going to make them want to head on over to your store and actually buy something. Also, a high bounce rate will make your credibility with Google and the other search engines go downhill.

Make Your Company an Expert in Your Field

If you want people to buy from your, make yourself an expert in the field you are in. For example, NAPA Auto Parts sells a lot of auto parts because people can go into any one of their parts stores and get expert advice on everything from which part they actually need to how to install it. If you are an expert in your niche, people will buy from you.

Develop a Unique Value Proposition

Having expertise in a field is important as is creating marketing that people will remember and a brand that they can put their trust in. But all of that is simply a precarious house of cards if you don't have anything of value to offer them. You want people to see the value in the products that you have, and that goes back to what we discussed in the first chapter – solving a problem for them.

Think of it this way: Imagine that you were sitting at your desk, with a ton of work to complete. Lunchtime rolled around and you were starving, but you didn't have time to go out and get something. Along comes a vendor selling a sandwich for $15. Sure, that's a pretty hefty price to pay for a sandwich, even a 12-inch sub sandwich, but you've got the money in your pocket and you're hungry, so you make the purchase. That's a unique value proposition. The vendor offered you something valuable that no one else was offering you.

Now imagine the same vendor coming along after you had ordered Chinese food delivery. You have already eaten and he comes along with his $15 sandwich. Not only do you not find value in his proposition, it is no longer unique, because another company has already met your need.

Cultivate Your "X-Factor"

Finally, you've heard of the "X-Factor." It is an indefinable quality that some companies have that makes people want to buy from them. There is no logic behind it like there are for more of the other items on this list. In fact, people often buy from an "X-Factor" company despite the lack of a good reason. Although cultivating that particular quality is difficult – because there are no instructions on how to do it, if you can pull it off you will be in a much more effective position to be successful at ecommerce.

Chapter Six:
Understanding Digital, Physical and Subscription Products

There are three different types of products that you can sell on Shopify – physical products such as clothes or electronics, digital products such as eBooks, music and software and subscription products where the consumer pays a monthly (usually) fee to be part of a program or have special access to digital products or information. Each one of these different types of product have their disadvantages and advantages and you don't necessarily have to choose just one. Many people sell multiple products types on their Shopify website. Which one or ones you choose will be up to you.

To make that decision easier, here are some of the things that you need to know about the different types of products that are out there. Understanding what goes into selling each type of product will help you determine what you are going to fill your Shopify store with. Let's start with the most common type of product sold on Shopify – the physical product.

Selling Physical Items on Shopify

Physical products are sold in Shopify stores all over the world. They range from computers, televisions and other big ticket items to items for the home, clothing, décor, jewelry and much more. Selling physical items on Shopify can be a rewarding and fulfilling experience, and it can certainly be a lucrative one. More people buy online these days than ever before in history and the number will continue to rise. But there are some disadvantages as well.

For one thing, when you sell physical products you have to worry about getting them to the consumer. At some point in the future, digital and physical objects may be intertwined, with information being sent to a 3D printer after a purchase which then creates the product in minutes or hours. For now, we still have to get items to people the old fashioned way and for your store that means shipping them using one of the services out there like the United States Postal Service, FedEx or UPS.

Something else that you have to consider when deciding whether or not to sell physical products is the problem of defective products, those that get damaged while being shipped to the consumer and other returns. You're going to need to create a return policy and then prepare for a certain percentage of returns. That percentage will be very low if you sell quality products, but no matter what, you are going to have returns.

With physical products you have the added disadvantage of having to buy them first, and keep a certain number in stock. There are some ways around that, which we'll discuss in Chapter Nine, but for most stores, you need to invest in inventory, and your profit margin will be much smaller than it is with digital products that you create. While you can sell a $20 eBook that costs you nothing to send to someone, with an unlimited amount of copies available to be sent, you will actually have to replace the physical inventory so you'll only be making your markup as profit.

Selling Digital Items on Shopify

The next type of product that we'll discuss is the digital product. A digital product is one in which it exists only in electronic form. There is no physical product to be shipped because the item is delivered electronically to the buyer. Digital items have become very popular in recent years. Even some items that used to be physical are now almost fully digital – or are at least offered as an option in digital format.

A good example of this is the eBook. It used to be that if you wanted to read a book, you either bought it from the bookstore or you checked it out from the library. Now, you can purchase the digital version of a book and read it instantly. Even libraries have gone digital, allowing you to check out the digital version of books and read them on your tablet, e-reader or smartphone, and return it when you are finished just as you would with a library book. But the eBook is only one type of digital product that you could sell, and since Amazon is the king of digital reading material, a book probably isn't the best choice for a product to sell anyway.

There are various other forms of digital product to be sold. One of the most common types today is the application or 'app' for smartphones and tablets. Apps for mobile devices are different than regular applications in two ways – one is that they are intended for use with a mobile device operating system like Android, rather than for a PC or Mac operating system, and second, they are made to be as small as possible because there is limited space on most mobile devices. However, computer software is also a viable digital product as are various website templates and more.

The four main types of digital product include the digital image, the mp3 or wav file, the software or application package and the digital video. All of these various media types are sold on the internet and make up nearly all of the digital products sold. Software includes games and popular programs like Microsoft Office and Skype, movies are streamed across the internet to Smart Televisions and iTunes has become one of the most popular digital music vendors of the 21st century. There is also a booming business in apps, with even small businesses paying to have their own app created.

As far as creating your own digital products, or selling digital products that you have the rights for, the potential for earning is high, since digital goods cost little to nothing to produce, at least after the initial manufacturing, and you can charge nearly as much as a comparable physical product if the demand is there. You'll have to decide if you have something digital that is worth selling on your Shopify site.

Selling Subscription Products on Shopify

The third type of item is the subscription product. Subscription products are those that are paid regularly and give access to a restricted area of some kind. For example, an application could be built into a website or downloaded that only allowed the person access if they had a current subscription. An example of this is a music service like Pandora, which offers both free and subscription based services. Netflix is a subscription based service that offers movies and television shows to subscribers. Gamefly is a subscription service that allows for the unlimited rental of video games and almost every stock photo website in existence has some sort of subscription service.

Choosing a subscription based model has a number of advantages for you. First, you don't just make money on the initial purchase. Instead, you get to make money each and every month that the person subscribes. Also, many people are able to set up a subscription service that only requires minimal maintenance which means that they are able to make money without doing very much work for it. However, you need to provide value to your customers in order to get them to subscribe and this can be a challenge.

Chapter Seven
Making Yourself a Niche Expert

One of the things that you are going to have to do to make yourself successful in your Shopify ecommerce efforts is to choose a niche and make yourself an authority for that niche. We'll explore what becoming an authority on a particular niche actually means and why it is so important to selling products, as well as some of the ways that you can do it. But first, let's define what a niche expert is.

What are Niche Experts?

When it comes to retail, niche experts are those websites where people go to buy products in that niche because they trust the niche expert. A niche expert is a website that ranks high in Google for particular niche keywords and who can be found being recommended on social media and word-of-mouth and who other websites link to when someone asked who they should ask a question about that niche. Niche experts are websites that have a reputation for knowing the niche that they are in and being able to provide not only great products in that niche, but also support for the products, recommendations and a high degree of trust.

Why Should You Make Yourself a Niche Expert?

Obviously, there are a number of advantages to become a niche expert but the most important one is that you will make more money. People want to buy from someone who is an expert in a particular niche. Many people would rather buy from a name that they know and trust rather than a site that sells just about everything. That's why there are people who still shop at Best Buy and other electronic stores online or buy their computer parts from Newegg rather than Amazon. They know that the retailer is an expert in the products that they are buying and can trust in their recommendations, or the products they have listed.

There are other reasons that you should make yourself an expert in your niche as well. For one thing, you'll rank higher as a result of the links that you get and the reputation you achieve as an authority site. Google will recognize this from various telltale signs, and will give you more ranking juice. Also, people will want to link to you, so you'll get traffic from those sources directly as well. Also, when you have an authority site, it is very easy to expand into other related areas. For example: if a website is considered an authority on shoes, they will rank higher and easier if they expanded into clothing than a new website that was devoted just to clothing would.

How to Make Your Shopify Site into a Niche Expert Site

So, how do you create an authority site within your niche that will give you all of the benefits mentioned in the last paragraph – being able to rank higher in Google, getting more links to your site and more sales because people consider you an authority? It isn't all that difficult but it does take some time and a great deal of hard work. There are two types of authority, page authority and domain authority, but for the purposes of ecommerce site you should be concentrating on domain authority.

Linking Strategies to Build Authority

The first thing you need to do if you want Google to consider you an authority site is to tell them what is it you do; they aren't going to ask so when the spiders come crawling you want to have your website's internal linking strategy in place where you can show Google what sort of topics you are an authority in.

You do this by creating strong bonds between the pages of your site. Each page should be optimized for a specific keyword or group or keywords and then linked to from deep links within your site. That means linking topics of the same type to each other. For example, if you have 10 products that are tools or hardware, on each page for those ten, you want to put something like a "related products" widget beneath it.

That's the great thing about Shopify: it makes tasks like this very easy to do. You should also create a page that lists all of the products within that particular topic and then make sure that Google knows this is your "Daddy" page for the child products that it lists by making sure that you link to that page 3-4 times more than you link to a specific product page.

These "Daddy" pages are going to become the authority figures of your site, with Google understanding that whatever topic these pages are about, that topic is something that your site might be an authority on. So, suppose your site was about hardware and you had a page for hammers and another for saws. You would be ranked more highly for hammers and saws than any other tool that comes up, even if you sell that particular tool. Also, make sure that you are linking to these "Daddy" pages from your 'About' page, contact page, footer or other areas in your site than just your product pages.

The next part of building your authority is getting links from outside sites – not owned or frequented by you – with the link containing keywords that are related to your site topic somehow. Now, you're going to get some of these naturally, especially if people think you know what you're talking about and can be trusted to recommend a product or service in that niche. But to begin with, you might have to send some of those links your way on your own. The way that you do that is by writing or publishing related content on other sites, or simply finding a site that is willing to link to you. Note that an inbound link doesn't mean much to Google if it doesn't come from a site that is related to your topic in some way, or is from a massive authority website.

Creating Video Content

Creating video content is another great way to get your name out there as well as get some traffic to your store. If you can make an expert video showing that you know what you're talking about, and it gets views on YouTube or another video-sharing site, you'll get traffic coming to your store, as long as you provide a link for them to navigate there. If you feel comfortable creating video content, this is a great way to go.

Google's Own Recommendations on Building an Authority Page

Google has actually recommended that you ask yourself these questions when trying to create an authority site. If the answer is NO to any of these questions, you probably need to fix it.

1. Is your content original, not like anything else on the web and definitely not plagiarized?
2. Is your advice practical? Are you advising people looking for a mortgage to get a "Construction for Dummies" book and build it themselves to save money?
3. Did you correct all of the misspellings, grammatical errors and typos?
4. Is the information that you're providing valuable? Providing obvious information will not make you an authority site.
5. Is the article cluttered?
6. Would you bookmark your page?

Chapter Eight
Laws, Regulations and Restrictions for Your Business & Your Products

There is a lot to think about when you are starting your ecommerce website and if you want to stay in business, understanding the laws and the regulations that govern your store is going to be paramount. There are six main areas that we're going to focus on when it comes to regulations, encompassing very different aspects of an ecommerce website. This information is based upon the laws that govern ecommerce websites that are based in the United States and the information may be different if you are starting your site elsewhere. In addition, there may be other regulations that govern your store if you are selling an unusual or regulated product.

Business Licensing

The first legality that we're going to discuss is your business license. Do you need to get one and how is that even accomplished? Let's start with what a business license actually is. A business license gives you the ability to operate a 'for profit' business in a certain area, usually a city or county. If you don't have a business license and you start a business, you can be fined and the city may force you to close your doors.

The business license is obtained through whatever city or county office gives them out in your area and each one will have different requirements or different types of licenses, which may or may not apply to an internet only business. The best thing to do is check with your local licensing office and get the current information for your city and state. You also should be aware that you cannot do business under that name until you are licensed, which means that banks aren't going to open a business account for you unless you can provide proof of your business name, commonly called a D.B.A.

Your Domain & Website Security

One of the reasons that you're going with Shopify is that it makes it much easier to build a store because most of the difficult stuff is already taken care of. That is the case with site security as well. Shopify has taken care of that aspect of your site for you, and in fact, is one of the most highly rated sites when it comes to security. As long as you're using the platform, chances of your store being hacked or your customer's financial information being stolen is extremely low.

However, there is one website-related thing that you're going to need to do, and that's register a domain. A domain will be the address where your store is located. It is an important decision because your domain will be the way that people find your store, and one of the ways that Google knows what your store is about.

Paying Taxes

Next, we'll discuss how taxes work. There are two different types of tax that you need to be aware of – sales tax and income tax. When you are in business for yourself, you are responsible for paying both of these on every item that you sell (usually) and every dollar that you make (almost).

Sales Tax: When you have an e-store, you actually don't have to pay sales tax on everything you sell. Your state only requires that you pay sales tax on items that you sell to people who live in your state, because a transaction from you to them means that you have "done business" in that state and that is subject to sales tax. When it comes to the other items that you sell, to people in other states, you don't have to pay sales tax so you only have to set up your store to charge sales tax to the people who live in your state.

Income Tax: The other type of tax that you'll have to pay is income tax. You remember when you used to get a tax refund check at the first of the year? Well, that time is over. Now, you'll be paying taxes on the income that you get because you don't have an employer to withhold those taxes for you. So, you'll need to set aside a portion of your income to pay taxes at the end of the year. If you set a certain percentage in a savings account, and the actual amount of taxes that you have to pay is less than what you have saved, then you do get a tax refund of sorts.

You won't know exactly what you have to pay until the end of the year because you get to deduct your expenses from your income and not pay taxes on any amount that you spent running your business. Your expenses can also include part of your rent, if you work from home, and even vehicle expenses if you had to drive anywhere for your business, such as to the post office to ship items. Any money that you spend running your business, that can be proven, you can deduct before you pay taxes. A tax advisor can help you make sure you get all of the deductions you deserve.

Hiring Employees

When it comes to hiring employees, there are several different laws that you'll need to familiarize yourself with. From income tax withholding to laws governing hiring policies, you'll need to check out the local regulations in your area as well as the federal labor laws. You may not think that you have need for employees right now, but if your business grows to the point where you can no longer keep up with the shipping, it is something that you might want to consider.

Here are some of the laws that you are going to have to familiarize yourself with if you decide to hire employees:

- Wage and hour regulations
- Workplace safety and health

- Worker's compensation
- Employee benefits and security
- Unions and their members
- Employee protection
- Regulations governing those in uniform
- The employee polygraph protection act
- Wage garnishment
- Family & medical leave law
- Special employment rights for veterans

Shipping Regulations

We're going to get into how to set up your shipping in a later chapter. For now, you should just be aware that there are some shipping regulations that govern how you need to label your packages, when you need insurance, what happens if you decide to ship overseas and the type of materials you are allowed to send through the U.S. mail or other shipper. For the most part, Shopify has already taken care of this for you with their shipping labels, so you can just concentrate on building your store and attracting customers.

Special Regulations

There are a few special regulations that you need to be aware of if you are running an ecommerce website. However, they are mostly to do with site security and protecting your customer's financial information, something that is taken care of by Shopify. There are also some rules governing online advertising that every e-store owner needs to review and then there could be special regulations governing your particular product as well. These are all things that you'll need to research and understand before you open your ecommerce site for the first time and before you make your first sale.

Part Two: Setting up Shopify

Chapter Nine
Where to Get Your Shopify Products

Unless you are planning to make your Shopify products yourself, such as jewelry or artwork, you are going to have to obtain your inventory somewhere. This can be challenging because not only do you need to find a reputable and reliable supplier of the inventory that you sell, you also need to be able to purchase it at a low enough price that you are able to make money on the product – commonly called buying wholesale. Buying wholesale is usually a lot easier if you are buying in bulk, and for a smaller ecommerce website, this might not be possible, particularly if you are selling big ticket physical products like electronics.

Of course, there are digital products to consider as well. Digital products can be a huge part of your income, particularly since if you create them yourself, you can sell them with no overhead whatsoever. Then, there are subscription products to consider, which might be something you add to your store if you have a valuable service that people are going to pay for month after month. But as far as obtaining products, let's start with where you can get your physical inventory.

Obtaining Items Wholesale

When an item is manufactured, ideally, it would go straight to retailers and then they could add their markup and sell the item in their store. Unfortunately, it doesn't happen like that at all. What actually happens is that the manufacturer sells it to a distributor, who then sells it to a wholesaler (or vice-versa) who then sells it to the retailer, if you're lucky. There may even be more middle-men with their hand out along the process and so the price can get pretty high by the time it gets to you.

The big stores like Walmart do enough business that they are able to skip a lot of steps and buy directly from the manufacturer. That's why they can offer their customers such low prices and be able to undercut the competition. But as an ecommerce website without any real clout, especially if you don't have the money to buy in bulk, you are going to be buying close to retail on some things. Some wholesalers won't sell to you unless you purchase a certain amount and others may not want to deal with you at all. Retailers often spend years building relationships with their suppliers in order to make sure they get the best price possible.

Where to Look to Buy Items Wholesale

If you want to buy items wholesale, you need to understand who the players are in your area. The wholesale industry has 50 of the biggest distributing companies generating a quarter of the income in the entire industry. The world of wholesale is a small one and there is a definite distribution chain that wholesalers supply through. It is a club that you have to have an invitation to be a part of.

At the highest level are the manufacturers who take the raw material and turn it into a product, or the import companies who buy it elsewhere and import it to the United States. Those companies then sell it to wholesalers or to distributers responsible for a region, and who distribute the product to the retail stores in that area. There are also brokers who are the go-between of small retail businesses and the distributors.

Volume & Relationships Mean Discounts

When it comes to getting the best price on items, you need to have one of two things, and probably both. You need to be buying large volumes of products, whether that be many items of the same product or just a large order, and you need to establish a relationship with your wholesaler. If you have been working with the same wholesaler for any length of time, you will begin to build a relationship, and that relationship will ensure that you get a good price down the road, even if you aren't necessarily buying as much inventory as they'd like to sell you, as they want to keep in your good graces.

Since you're new, it is unlikely that you're going to have a relationship with the supplier so you're going to have to work towards it, and make up for it by buying in bulk as often as you can. Even so, there are wholesalers who will sell and ship to small businesses if you look for them. You may not get as good of price from these wholesalers but as you become more and more well-known in supplier circles you will be able to move up the ladder to get to a better supplier.

Where to Look for Wholesalers

The best place for you to look for wholesalers these days is probably the internet, as you don't know anyone outside of the web that you can call. There are definitely wholesalers who list online and market themselves to businesses via the web. There are also trade associations and directories that you can make use of like Wholesale Central. One way that you can go about finding the right supplier online is to find a store that sells some of same products that you do and shoot them an email to ask for a recommendation. They may not wish to help you if they are a competitor of yours, so try to find someone who you're not competing with.

Other than the internet, you can find wholesalers by attending trade shows. There are dozens and possibly hundreds of trade shows that have wholesalers attending them and if you can attend you may be able to get a supplier that you wouldn't have ordinarily had access to. You can also read trade magazines, particularly the classifieds section, to find wholesales that supply your particular product. You can also get recommendations from business organizations like the SBA, Small Business Development Center and the local chamber of commerce.

You might also want to try talking to the manufacturer themselves. Although you probably aren't going to get them to sell you products at the prices they sell to wholesalers, they might give you some recommendations of the people farther down the supply chain that serves small businesses. Another great idea is to visit retailer forums, particularly those for ecommerce.

Of course, there is always the Amazon affiliate program as well.

Getting Digital Products to Sell

Depending upon what the digital product is that you are planning to sell, you can almost always make good money on them. You might have heard of Clickbank as the digital marketplace for sellers and affiliates. The problem with clickbank products is that they are often overpriced because the creator doesn't sell that many and has to be an affiliate commission whenever they do sell something. However, Clickbank isn't the only game in town.

Figure out what sort of digital product that you'd like to sell, and whether you plan on providing that digital product yourself or whether you plan to be an affiliate for someone else and then search the internet for products that fit your needs. You'll probably have to do some real research, because once you find a product, you need to vet it carefully, but soon you'll have some digital inventory to sell.

Chapter Ten
Choosing the Right Shopify Package

When you start selling with Shopify, there are different packages that you'll be choosing from in order to use the platform to sell your products or services. Choosing the right package is important because it will determine what sort of features you get with your store and the tools that you'll have at your disposal to run your business. The easiest way to allow you to determine what package you should go with is to describe each feature that Shopify offers, based upon this chart, and then mark which membership tiers get access to that feature.

At the time of this writing, the Shopify plans are as follows:

Lite: $9 per month
Basic: $29 per month
Pro: $79 per month
Unlimited: $179 per month

Features Offered by Shopify with Membership

Online Store: Basic, Pro, Unlimited

With Shopify, this is where everything begins. If you want to have an online store, you need to choose one of the membership plans that offer it – Basic, Pro or Unlimited. If you choose the Lite plan, you aren't going to get a store.

Point-of-Sale: Lite, Basic, Pro, Unlimited

You get the point-of-sale feature with all of the plans. What this gives you is the ability to take payments any way you need to using the Shopify POS. That means that you can accept payments in both the virtual and real world and it is easy to set up with an app on your mobile device and an intuitive design that requires no training whatsoever. There is also a retail add-on package that gives you everything you need to sell in a brick-and-mortar store.

Facebook Integration: Lite, Basic, Pro, Unlimited

With this feature you store gets fully integrated with Facebook so when people visit your page, they can see the items that you have in your store, updated whenever you change them, and be able to click through to your store and buy if they want to. No matter which plan you choose you get this integration.

Pinterest Integration: Basic, Pro, Unlimited

This feature comes with every package except for the Lite package and it allows you to sell items from your store directly on Pinterest buy having a buy button integrated into your pins. Buyable pins allow customers to buy without even leaving Pinterest and could definitely result in a lot more sales.

Twitter Integration: Basic, Pro, Unlimited

Again, comes with every package except for the Lite, and this feature works pretty much the same as the Pinterest integration does. Anytime you tweet a product, it will automatically include a buy button, product image and description so that people can shop without even leaving Twitter.

Shopify Buy Button: Lite, Basic, Pro, Unlimited

The Shopify buy button is how you can add your buy button to any website that you choose, and it comes with all of the different packages that Shopify offers.

Retail Package: Lite, Basic, Pro, Unlimited

This is the cost of the retail add-on package. With some features, you get a discount with the higher priced Shopify packages, but with this particular one, the retail add-on costs $40 no matter which package you go with.

Credit Card Rates: Lite, Basic, Pro, Unlimited

As mentioned in the last feature, some tiers give you different costs. This is an example of those. You pay less fees for accepting credit cards the higher of a tier you choose. So for the Lite and Basic packages, you pay 2.9% plus 30 cents online and 2.7% plus 0 cents in person while the Pro package only charges you 2.6% plus 30 cents online and 2.4% plus 0 cents in person. The Unlimited package gives you a further discount – 2.4% plus 30 cents online and 2.2% plus 0 cents in person.

Transaction Fees: Lite, Basic, Pro, Unlimited

So, for this package, you don't pay any transaction fees with Shopify Payments no matter which package you choose. But if you use external payment gateways you are going to pay 2% on the Lite and Basic packages, and 1% with the Pro. The Unlimited package only charges you half a percent transaction fees on outside payments.

Number of Products: Lite, Basic, Pro, Unlimited

No matter which package you go with, you get an unlimited number of products in your store.

24/7 Support: Lite, Basic, Pro, Unlimited

All of the packages include 24/7 support. If you are paying for a package with Shopify, you get access to support 24 hours a day, 7 days a week, 365 days per year.

Shipping Label Discounts: Lite, Basic, Pro, Unlimited

When you buy shipping labels from Shopify you get deeper discounts with the higher tier packages. With Lite and Basic, you get up to 50% off shipping labels while you get another 5% off with Pro and another 10% off (for a total of up to 60% off) with Unlimited

Fraud Analysis: Lite, Basic, Pro, Unlimited

No matter what package you go with you get Shopify's award-winning fraud analysis to make sure that you are protected from fraudulent purchases.

Manual Order Creation: Lite, Basic, Pro, Unlimited

Again, you get this feature no matter which package you choose. What a manual order feature gives you is the ability to enter an order manually without having the customer purchase the product online. That means if you sell something in the real world you can still take advantage of Shopify's features by entering it into the system manually.

Website & Blog: Basic, Pro, Unlimited

With the exception of the Lite package, you get to have a website and blog through Shopify with any of the tiers that you choose. This allows you to blog and builds authority as well as gives you an ecommerce store. Blogging can help you rank for more keywords as well.

File Storage: Lite, Basic, Pro, Unlimited

No matter what you choose here, you get unlimited file storage.

Discount Codes: Lite, Basic, Pro, Unlimited

Discount codes allow you to run promotions and give your customers a discount when they use a specific code. This is a very good tool for knowing where your traffic came from and which advertising methods work the best.

Gift Cards: Basic, Pro, Unlimited

With the Basic, Pro and Unlimited packages you get gift cards that your customers can use to give to other people or use at a later date.

Professional Reports: Pro, Unlimited

The Pro and the Unlimited packages are the only ones that give you the ability to run advanced reports and see what is really going on in your store. You do get some basic reporting without this feature, but it is very limited and it could be worth upgrading to the Pro or Unlimited packages all by itself.

Abandoned Cart Recovery: Pro, Unlimited

This allows customers to come back after closing out the page and finding their shopping cart just as they left it.

Advanced Report Builder: Unlimited

The only package that you get this advanced report builder in is the Unlimited package and in fact, this is one of only two features that you can only get with the Unlimited package.

Real Time Carrier Shipping: Unlimited

This is the other feature that you get only with the Unlimited package.

Chapter Eleven
Shopify compared to other ecommerce platforms

If you are considering using Shopify, you might be wondering whether they live up to their claim as the best ecommerce platform or whether there is a better solution out there. To help you answer that question, this chapter will go over some of the top ecommerce platforms and discuss the advantages and disadvantages of each one, as well as how they stack up to Shopify.

An Ecommerce Platform Defined

The first thing that we'll do is define what an ecommerce platform actually is. An ecommerce platform is a software program that gives you the framework to build an online store. This means that rather than having to code in things like product pages, shopping carts, buying buttons and various other complex design elements. All of that is done for you when you use an ecommerce platform. All you have to do is customize your site with the design that you want – usually through the use of themes, and then add your products and other information. It is an easy way to build an online store as long as you choose a platform that does what you need it to do.

Comparison: Shopify Against Other Platforms

There are many ecommerce platforms out there to choose from – hundreds if not thousands. Shopify is by far the most popular and the most widely used of all of these platforms but does that mean it is the best? We'll be looking at the top ecommerce platforms and see how Shopify stacks up against each of them. If Shopify is the best, you should know why, and be able to compare the platform fairly against all of the others in order to make an informed, unbiased decision. So, let's compare them one by one.

The Top Ecommerce Platforms

We'll be comparing Shopify against three platforms that are definitely up there in the top five with Shopify: Magento, Bigcommerce and Volusion. We'll compare each one with Shopify on the basis of the following factors: Pricing, design customization, features, security, marketing, reports, add-ons and support. These are all of the basic framework components of each ecommerce platform out there and by looking at these eight factors you can decide how each of them compare with Shopify and decide which one you are going to go with, or if you are still going to use Shopify.

Pricing

First, let's discuss pricing. Magento is free unless you want to upgrade to the Enterprise Edition, which is pretty pricey. BigCommerce is the most expensive of the bunch with four tiers of features, each one about double what Shopify costs per month. Volusion and Shopify are very similar when it comes to pricing.

Design Customization

Next is design customization. All of these design customizations are based upon themes. All of the platforms have some free themes and then there are premium themes as well. BigCommerce doesn't charge anything for their selection of 100 themes, but the quality is pretty low. Volusion has a couple of dozen free themes and then nearly a hundred premium ones, and the quality is comparable to Shopify. Magento has some free themes but most of the good ones are premium and they can run upwards of $150. Shopify and Volusion definitely have the best out of the four and Shopify themes are a little higher quality.

Frontend Features

These four are nearly comparable when it comes to frontend features. The only problem really lies with the BigCommerce platform which isn't very clean. It does have more features than any other platform to make up for it however. All of the frontend designs are mobile responsive so you don't have to worry about that.

Backend Features

BigCommerce is the clear winner here when it comes to backend features. There is just enough customization to allow you to make your store look the way you want and the interface is very nice and clean. Shopify also has a clean interface and is fairly robust although not quite as nice as BigCommerce. Both Volusion and Magento have backends that have a very steep learning curve and although Magento offers a much greater array of features, it is almost impossible for first-time users to make the backend do what they want without learning much of the tutorial information first.

Security

Shopify is the clear winner here because of the hosting that they offer and the fact that they feature a Content Delivery Network (CDN) and are PCI compliant. BigCommerce is pretty secure as well but doesn't feature a CDN. Volusion does provide hosting and have a CDN and PCI compliance but you have to pay for encryption which Shopify offers for free. Magento requires that you get outside hosting which costs you extra per month, but the basic edition of Magento is free to make up for it.

Marketing

The marketing encompasses several aspects including SEO, social media and more. When it comes to SEO the big winner is BigCommerce as the SEO customization is very well planned and quite robust. Shopify only has the basic SEO features and Volusion is even worse. However, Magento has everything built in for SEO just the way you'd need it.

As for social media integration, all of them are about the same except for Magento, which offers no social media integration whatsoever. As for the newsletter feature, both Volusion and Magento have them built in. Shopify and BigCommerce doesn't have a built-in newsletter but they do integrate easily with third-party application for this feature.

All of the platforms offer the same basic promotion features like discounts and coupon codes. They also all support selling items via other channels and allow you to use the onsite marketing tools to start bringing in traffic.

Reports

As for reports, they all offer pretty much the same thing. The reports and statistics features on these platforms are all basically the same and give you the much-needed information about conversion rates, bounce rates and an overview of the products that you are selling. There is no real clear winner here when it comes to this feature.

Add-ons

All of these platforms also offer add-ons that will extend the usability of the platform and give you even more features than you had before. They have app sections of each platform that you can browse and decide how you want to expand your store. The thing about the apps is that they are constantly changing and each platform is always moving alongside the others so you can't really pick a clear winner based on this. What you have to do instead is decide which one you are going to use and then keep track of the add-ons that you see.

Support

Okay, so what about support? Let's start with Shopify. No matter what package you choose – including the $9 a month Basic package you get 24/7 support. BigCommerce has a great education center and you can get in touch with support 24/7 weekdays and between limited hours on the weekends. Volusion offers phone, live chat and email support 24/7 and then Magento is the one that is seriously lacking in support unless you upgrade to the expensive Enterprise version. However, you can visit forums to get help with Magento .

Chapter Twelve
Your Initial Setup

This chapter is intended to guide you through the initial setup of your Shopify store. Although every effort has been made to ensure accuracy, things may be a slightly different when you read this, since Shopify could change the way their platform works at any time. However, it should allow you to set up your site even if the instructions have changed because Shopify is one of the most intuitive and easy-to-use platforms out there.

Let's start with the initial sign-up if you haven't already done it. You can sign up easily by going to http://www.shopify.com. At the time of this writing, the platform offers a fourteen day trial that will allow you to explore and test out the interface without spending a dime. When you visit the site for the first time, and you click the free trial button right in the center, you will only need to enter three pieces of information to get started: your name, your email and your store name. Don't worry – if you want to change the name of your store later on, you are free to do so from the 'Settings' page.

Getting Started: The Shopify Interface

The great thing about the Shopify interface is that it is very similar to Wordpress, a platform that most people are already familiar with. It includes the same backend design where you would normally create pages and posts with Wordpress. In this case, you are managing your orders, adding products and changing your settings. So, your initial interface has the following sections on the left-hand sidebar.

Search: This is the first item on your sidebar – a universal search function that allows you to find just about anything within your site, including a specific customer, a certain product or even blog posts that you have made.

Home: This button simply takes you back to your initial "home" page within the backend interface.

Orders: The third item on your sidebar list is the 'Orders' section and it has three subsections within the orders page. You can take a look at any abandoned carts as well as any actual orders that have come in. You also have a 'Drafts' section that will allow you to send orders from your admin page as well as invoices and more.

Products: Next up are the products that make up your store. We'll get into products in much more detail in the next chapter, but as a basic overview you have a place for you to add products to your store, a place to manage inventory, and get detailed reporting on your stock, a place where you can transfer and track incoming products, a section for gift cards and a section for collections.

Customers: One of the major benefits that Shopify has over other ecommerce platforms is just how much information you get and this section is a perfect example of that. You can keep track of all of your customers with this feature, allowing you to instantly see someone's name, past purchases, pertinent information like location and this section even stores a picture for you so that you can recognize them if you are meeting them face-to-face for the first time.

Reports: Again, Shopify is so powerful specifically because of features like this. You have the ability to run reports on almost any aspect of your business and you'll be able to see everything clearly and understand how your marketing efforts are going, what products are moving and which ones are selling too slowly as well as a number of other options. Here are some of the nearly two dozen different types of reports that you can run.

- Visitors by referral site
- Visitors based upon what kind of device they are using
- Visitors by location
- Analysis of shopping habits and carts
- Tax reports
- Payment methods
- Sales for a month, hour or by customer as well as several other powerful sales reports

Discounts: The next section that we'll look at is discounts section where you can create promotional codes and rewards programs in order to get customers to return to your store or to track various promotional channels and determine which marketing efforts are the most effective. You can create any sort of promotional code you want and three are three different ways that you can give them a discount.

First, you can give them a percentage discount which means that they get a certain percentage off of their entire purchase. You specify what the percentage will be and then decide whether they get that percentage off of the entire amount, or a percentage off of orders of a certain amount or over. You can also specify a percentage discount for a specific group of products or for one specific product. Finally, you can give an individual customer a discount.

The second type of discount that you can do is a discount dollar amount. Rather than give customers a percentage off, you can give them a specific amount of money off of a product and again, you have various options as to where you want them to be able to apply this discount, including orders over a certain dollar amount, for a particular product or category or for an Individual customer.

Finally, you can do a free shipping discount which applies to orders over a certain amount and can be customized for the U.S. only, non-US shipping or anywhere in the world. Promo codes can also have a certain number of times they can be used so if you only want the first 100 people to get a working promo code for example, and you can set the dates that your promo codes can be used.

The next sidebar section is the 'Online Store' which is a series of settings that control your store being launched, the theme that you choose and how it is configured, your blog posts that work side-by-side with your store, the way that your navigation is set up and the domains that you have being directed to host your store, including subdomains or forwarding domains.

The Apps setting will give you two options. The first is the option to see what apps you already have installed and to configure them each individually, similar that the way that plugins work with Wordpress. You can also visit the Shopify app store which doesn't just contain apps that are created by Shopify, but is actuall sort of an 'open source' bype area where anyone can create an app that can then be installed on your Shopify site. Many of the apps listed here are free, but others cost anywhere from a dollar or two to twenty dollars or more.

Finally, there is the settings area, which allows you to set everything from the name of your store (if you want to choose a different name) to setting up your payment details and choosing what type of payment option you are going to use for your store. You can also set up all of your standard ecommerce options like which states you are going to choose sales tax in and how much that sales tax will be. You'll also configure your shipping options here and we'll get into most of the items in this area in a different chapter.

Chapter Thirteen
Adding Products to Your Store

The task of adding your products to your store will take up the bulk of your time unless you can find a way to automate the process somewhat. There are things that you can do to speed up the adding of products, such as importing your inventory using a CSV file, and we'll get into that as well. The goal of this chapter is to make it as easy and painless as possible to get your items added into your store along with the proper information for shipping, pricing and categorization. This is going to be a step-by-step guide that will cover all aspects of adding products, since it is arguably the most important part of having an ecommerce website.

Exploring the Products Section

The first thing that we'll do is a quick overview and exploration of the products section of your Shopify store. There are two basic parts that you need to be aware of. The first is the tutorial section, where you can learn through text instructions and screenshots, exactly how you can create your products, and the actual section where you add and edit your products, as well as do other related tasks.

The Help Section

In order to get to your tutorial section, you simply click on 'Products' from your admin page and then scroll down to click the link at the bottom that says 'Learn more about products.' This will take you to the visual tutorial that will teach you everything that you need to know. Let's go through the tutorial section quickly so that you can understand where to get help when you need it. There are nineteen separate sections that pertain to products in the help section, which is actually part of the entire Shopify manual. Another way that you can access it, without having to go to the products page first, is to type in docs.shopify.com and then when the help section comes up, simply clicking on the 'manual' link.From there you'll be able to access the massive amount of help information that Shopify provides to you on everything from products to gift cards.

Introduction to Adding Products

So, what exactly are products? They are the items that are for sale in your store. You have specific products that have their own images and you may have a particular quantity as well. The adding or a product is a four-step process.

- Step One: Adding a product title, which works much in the same way as adding a Wordpress post.
- Step Two: Adding images for that product. You can add more than one, but you'll also have a primary product image.
- Step Three: Adding a product description. While the title should describe your product, the description will be what actually sells your product to the customer.

- Step Four: Create variations of your product. For example, you might have different sizes, different colors or other variants.

Adding Your First Product

In order to add your first product you are going to have to navigate back to the Shopify admin page, assuming you are within the help section. The easiest ways way to do is just to enter www.shopify.com in your address bar and then press enter. It will take you back to the admin page. From there, click on the products link on the sidebar and you will be able to add a new product.

First, click on 'Product' and then click on the large blue button that says 'Add Product.' This will take you a a entry page that looks very much like a Wordpress 'add new post' page. You'll need to completely the following information if you want to add your product to your store.

1. Title: For example if you were starting a clothing store, this would be where you would put a specific style of tee shirt. For example: 'plain tee-shirts.' You don't want to add additional information like size or color just yet.
2. Next is your product description. This is where you'll type in the information that will sell this item to a potential customer. For example:

   "These 100% cotton T-shirts are comfortable and stylish, and make the perfect complement to slacks and a belt, to protect the skin from suspenders and go underneath dress shirts for formal occasions. "

3. Next, you want to add your product images. You can add more than one image if you want, but you should try to be selective and only add images that are necessary to show a different aspect of your item – for example: a different color. Also, you can include image alternative text which will help both for SEO purposes and to describe the image if it won't display for some reason.
4. On the right sidebar at the top you'll see the visibility, which is where you want the product to be seen (i.e. the main store) and the visible date, which is simply the date that you are lunching that product. This will probably be the same day you launch your store, but sometimes, people have a product coming out on a specific day.
5. Next, you'll fill in your organization information. This means that you'll identify where in your organization tree this item fits. For example: If it is a t-shirt, it probably fits within the 'shirts' category. You'll further identify it by creating a vendor. This is a useful tool not only for organizing your products, but also for keeping of which of your vendors this product belongs to so that you can order it again when it gets sold. If you are doing consignment this is also helpful.
6. The last item on the sidebar is the collections search tool so that you can add it to item collections that will help your customers find items within specific collections and could help you make more sales by giving visitors something else to look at after they have checked out this item.

7. At the bottom, you'll decide on the price of the product and then choose a price to compare it to. This is simply a way for you to create a sales price, with the "Compare at" price being the original, regular price, and the selling price being what you are selling the item for "now," That way, you can show a higher "original" price so that customers will think that the price has been slashed. You can also check the box that will tell the website to charge tax on that particular item, no matter what the location of the person buying it.
8. You'll set your inventory tracking numbers in the next two boxes. Your first will be your SKU or 'Stock Keeping Unit' and other will be your barcode, or in the case of a book, your International Standard Book Number (ISBN).
9. In the next section, you'll add in shipping weight using ounces, pounds, kilograms or grams and set up any international tariff codes that apply.
10. Near the bottom ou'll get to the most powerful part of the product listing – the variants. You choose the name of each variant, such as size, color, etc., and you'll set a variant value for each of the variants that you create to apply to this particular product, which will then apply to similar products as well.
11. The last part of the main product listing is the SEO preview, which will allow you to see the HTML title and description that you have created as well as set website SEO options if necessary.

Product Transfers

Another extremely powerful feature that the product listing or "Add Product" page includes is the ability to manage transfers. Transfers make it extremely easy to track and update your incoming inventory by letting Shipfy keep track for you. You set this up in your item listings by clicking the 'edit' link in the variants section. Go down to the inventory section and choose "Shopify tracks this product's inventory" from the dropdown. After you have set the product to be tracked by Shopify you can create a transfer.

You do this by clicking the second option in the product sidebar (Products, Transfers, Inventory, etc.) You'll record the incoming inventory from a supplier (note: this is not the brand or vendor information that we created earlier. This is where you actually purchase the product whereas vendor is more likt he brand of the item). Once you have arrived at the transfers page, click 'Add Transfer' and choose your supplier (or create a new one if necessary). You'll also fill out the arrival date of your inventory transfer. Find the items that you are going to be receiving in that transfer order and take special care to get the quantities right because you can't change them once the inventory date arrives. When you have entered in all of the products that you will be receiving in that particular delivery you simply save it.

Inventory Tracking, Collections & Gift Cards

Once you have inventory entered into your database, you will be able to view it and track it at a glance by clicking on the third option in the products section – inventory. You'll be able to accept or reject items from a supplier once the date has arrived for the order to get there and you can also click on the fourth option on the list to view your collections including being able to see any collections that you have created and get a birds-eye view of that particular part of your store. You'll also be able to set up gift cards for sale in that section as well which will give customers virtual gift cards to purchase.

Chapter Fourteen
Setting Up Your Shipping

Two of the important aspects of your ecommerce store are shipping and taxes. You will need to create shipping policies and determine what company you are going to use to do your shipping. You may need to offer more than one. Whatever you choose, you will also need to set up the options to work with your products so that your customers can choose the shipping options that they prefer. You don't want to just have one shipping policy. Sometimes, your customers may be willing to pay extra to have their item delivered as soon as possible and a store that offers multiple shipping options that customers want is going to earn the loyalty of those customers.

The Various Shipping Options

There are several different options that you have when it comes to shipping. What you choose will depend entirely upon what sort of items you are selling, what you think your customers will prefer and what is going to be most cost-effective for you. Let's go over the four different shipping options that you have to choose from when planning out your store.

Manual Shipping Rates

The first of the four options is manual shipping. In manual shipping you set the rates yourself and use whatever shipping services that you want to offer to customers, or even offer customer pickup in lieu of shipping. The advantage that this method has is that you can easily add in incidental costs or handling fees, which are sometimes necessary depending upon what it is you are planning on shipping. The disadvantage of this method is that the calculated costs are usually more than customers expect to pay for shipping and it will not match up if they decide to check on the shipping costs themselves, nor do you have the flexibility to ship a variety of different weights, sizes and the like.

For example, with manual shipping you might set a shipping cost that is based upon the expected weight of an item but if the item weighs more than you anticipating you will be paying the extra shipping cost yourself. On the other hand, if you charge a customer for shipping something and the weight is less than you anticipating, it will likely cost you less to ship, allowing you to pocket the difference, but your customers may not be happy with the price that they paid for shipping. Finally, you have the disadvantage of almost having to set up shipping costs for every product if you have a wide variety of sizes and weights because it can be difficult to calculate weight and dimensions across a wide variety of shipments.

The only time that this is the best option to choose is when you require special handling fees because of the products that you are shipping and all of your products are basically the same size and weight. So, you can set a standard shipping cost of $5 or $10 or whatever you choose to use as your manual shipping rate. Of course, if you don't have a shipping option and you simply want to charge a handling fee for customer pickup this is the best option to choose for that because you can set it at a standard handling amount. Many store owners also use this for charging a delivery fee within their local delivery area.

Shopify USPS Shipping

The standard shipping method used by Shopify is USPS or the United States Postal Service. If you are sealing a variety of items, with various dimensions and weights, this can be a very useful option. For one thing, you get the benefit of reduced rate shipping because you are using it with Shopify. Another advantage that this method has is that you can set it up almost instantly without any real configuration. The only thing that you need to set up yourself is the weight and dimensions of your products. The Shopify USPS shipping option works very similar to the one offered by Ebay, so if you have ever sold anything on that ecommerce site, you probably already know how it works.

In case you have never sold anything on Ebay or aren't familiar with how their shipping policies work, here is an overview of Shopify's USPS standard shipping program. You enter the dimensions of the shipping container that you are going to be transporting your items in, and come as close as you can to the weight (after) being placed in the shipping container, and Shopify will offer your customers various shipping options depending upon how fast they want their order to arrive. The options that they will see will depend upon several factors, such as the type of item being shipped, the size, dimensions and weight, and the particular type of shipping being offered at that time.

There are several major benefits to using this option instead of any of the others. The benefit for your customers is that they can see exactly what the shipping is going to cost them and they can choose the shipping that they want and are willing to pay for. The benefit for you, the merchant, is that when you use Shopify's USPS shipping and print their labels, you get a discount on the shipping cost.

Remember in the comparison of the different payment tiers offered by Shopify? One of the factors that were affected by which tier you chose was how much you would pay for the shipping. With the Basic option for $29 a month, you got a 50% discount on shipping labels. An upgrade to the Professional plan for $79 a month gave you a 55% discount on shipping labels and the $179 Unlimited plan gave you a 60% discount on labels. So, you can see that there is a direct correlation between what you pay and what you save when it comes to shipping and if you can estimate how much shipping you'll be doing, you can calculate which plan to go with based on shipping costs alone. Of course, there are other features that come with the higher tier plans as well.

Shipping Costs Calculated by the Carrier

UPS and FexEx, as well as a few other shipping companies, will provide you with a shipping API that will allow you to calculate real-time shipping costs for those shipping services. Obviously, this is a major benefit to customers who prefer a different shipping method than USPS or who can save money by shipping their purchase with FedEx or another shipper but this method has a decided disadvantage for you in that you have to choose the Unlimited plan to be able to use it. Of course, if you are choosing the Unlimited plan because you are going to be shipping enough USPS to warrant the extra cost than it would make sense to offer additional shipping options as well. You won't get the discount on any UPS or FedEx shipments however.

Drop-Shipping or Fulfillment Services

The fourth type of shipping option that you will have access to is that of a drop-shipper or fulfillment service. This is where you sell products that are then shipped to the buyer by the person you are buying the products from – your supplier. So, your supplier will charge you a certain amount, which may or may not include shipping, and you will set your rates by this cost. The advantage that this method has – besides the advantage of not having to warehouse your products of course – is that you can charge a specific price on all of your products and offer "free" shipping to your customers. The best way to make use of this method is in much the same way that Amazon and Walmart does – where they offer free shipping when you order a certain amount. If a customer chooses not to order that amount, you can calculate a manual rate to charge them but in most cases, they will order the minimum amount that qualifies for free shipping as long as it is reasonable, which means you make more money off of that customer.

How to Set Up Your Shipping Options

All of your shipping options are configured in the 'Settings' menu. You begin by navigating to settings and then clicking on 'Shipping.' We'll go through the ways that you configure these options step-by-step.

The first part that we'll cover is the return address that you'll be using. By default, Shopify fills in the name of your store (which you may have chosen in haste and want to change later one since it is the first thing that they make you choose) and the address and telephone number that you entered when you signed up, which might be your home address and mobile number. Obviously, you may not want this information on your shipping labels. Many ecommerce websites uses post office boxes that they rent and many smaller companies do not have contact telephone numbers at all. Luckily, Shopify allows you to easily change this information by clicking the EDIT ADDRESS link and entering in new information.

Shipping Zones – Manual Shipping

If you want to set up manual shipping you can do it with the shipping zones section of your shipping options. You'll have two basic options – domestic and the rest of the world. Within your domestic shipping zones, which you can set to be whatever countries or states that you choose, you can set a standard shipping amount and a heavy shipping amount. You can set other shipping rates that you choose as well, based upon weight or based upon price.

With the 'rest of the world' option you only get several shipping rates as well. As discussed, this gives you a little freedom when it comes to your shipping costs and configuring them for multiple sizes and weights but is still rather restrictive compared to other shipping options. .

Shipping – Carrier Calculated

If you have an unlimited plan, then you can use carrier calculated shipping. Shopify doesn't give you the option to configure that until you have upgraded your plan, but once you do, you can enter the API information and get shipping details directly from the carrier.

Shipping – Shopify Shipping & Labels

If you want to use Shopify shipping labels and shipping services you have two options to configure in the shipping section of your admin area. The first is setting up the printer that you are going to use to print labels on. This is important because the Shopify labels will only print out on certain printers.

The second part of the Shopify shipping is defining various package sizes so that Shopify can set a price. You'll be able to set a product type like 'box' and then create dimensions that will define what sort of prices are shown when the customer chooses a particular product.

Finally, there are options to connect a drop shipping service. If you are doing order fulfillment through a third-party company, it is easy to set them up to work with Shopify. By default, Shopify supports Shipwire, Rakuten and Amazon order fulfillment. However, you can create custom order fulfillment as well if you choose. You do this via email, by specifying where customer information should be sent when someone places an order so that the fulfillment company can then send the order to the customer. However, the three fulfillments services supported by Shopify have more features and custom configuration that can be done.

Chapter Sixteen
Customizing Your Payment Solutions & Taxes

When you have configured your shipping and taxes on Shopify, the next thing that you'll move onto is your payment solutions. From the payments page, you can set up multiple payment options and decide just how you are going to take payments. As with shipping, there are payment options that are offered by Shopify itself, and fees are again based upon your tier choice, as well as a number of other payment options. We'll discuss all of the choices that you have for accepting payments and which ones are best for the type of selling that you will be doing. First, let's get to the page where you configure your payment options.

Customizing Your Payment Solutions

You can navigate to the page where the payment options may be set by clicking on the gear icon and clicking on payments. There are several payment options that are integrated right into Shopify and options to set up other payment methods as well.

Shopify Payments

Shopify Payments is the first option on the list and it is definitely the easiest way to accept payments with a Shopify store. However, Shopify Payments cannot be used everywhere. It is available only in the UK, Australia, the United States and Canada. Shopify Payments is easy to set up and removes the need for a third-party gateway, and has more credit card acceptance options than many other payment systems and it comes fully integrated into your store.

Benefits of Using Shopify Payments

- You can accept all major credit cards including American Express, Visa and MasterCard debit and credit cards. In addition, if your store is based in the United States, you can accept Diner's Club, JCB and Discover cards as well.
- You decide what credit card fees you are going to pay by the Shopify plan that you select.
- You can see when your next payout is and how much is expected at any time via your Shopify admin area.
- Shopify provides solutions to help you avoid and respond to chargebacks.
- Shopify charges no additional fees other than the percentage fees that are part of your payment plan.
- PCI Compliance fees are already included in your credit card processing fees.

How to Configure Shopify Payments

There are a few things that you need to configure if you are going to use Shopify Payments. First, you need to decide if you want Shopify to notify you whenever you receive a payment. This will be done via email. Next, you need to decide upon what security precautions you are going to use to prevent fraud. There are two standard debit or credit card security options that can be used with Shopify Payments in every country except Australia, in which neither can be used. The first verification is the CVV – the three digit number on the back of the card. The second verification is the address verification where the zip code needs to match the address on file for the credit or debit card. You can choose to turn these verifications off, but you will have no fraud prevention and may receive orders on stolen credit card numbers.

You'll also need to enter some additional information like a store name and telephone number that will appear on the billing statements of the credit cards of your customers. You'll also need to add your bank account and choose the currency that you want your store to be based upon.

Paypal

You can also set up your store to accept Paypal payments. What you need to keep in mind here is that you must have a Paypal merchant account in order to take payments through Shopify. However, you don't have to set it up the first time that you launch the site. In fact, you can set up Paypal payments on your site and only create a merchant account once you have actually received a Paypal payment, so you can always have it offered, but not necessarily need to use it.

One thing that you do want to be aware of if you decide that you are going to set up Paypal payments on your Shopify store is that if you want to be able to process Paypal refunds or accept payments automatically you are going to need to deactivate the default Paypal account that is included and then re-activate it. This will allow you full use of the Paypal function. You do this by clicking the gear icon and going to Settings and then clicking on Payments. From there, you will see the Paypal function in your payment options. Then click Edit, Deactivate and then choose your Paypal type and select Reactivate.

Amazon Payments

The next payment method that you have to choose from is Amazon Payments. This is a well-known method for making purchases using the payment information and shipping details that they already have in their Amazon account. There are only three countries that are eligible for Amazon Payments with a Shopify store: The United States, the United Kingdom and Germany.

To activate Amazon Payments there are three steps that need to be taken. First, you need to register your merchant account with Amazon. You'll start in the Amazon Payments section, and click Activate to take you to the Amazon page where you can set up your account. If you already have an account, you don't need to register a new one. Instead, just enter your login information on the Amazon Payments site. Otherwise, there is the option to create a new login.

Now, you'll want to configure your account using the link in your Shopify store. When you configure your account, it will give you the keys that you need to use with you Shopify store. The next thing you'll need to do is set up 'Login with Amazon.' This has to be done from your store, so it might be prudent to go back to your store admin and navigate once again to your Amazon Payments account from your Shopify admin page.

Once you arrive back at Amazon, look at the top menu bar and use the dropdown to select "Login with Amazon" and then click "Create Application." Enter the name of your application. This will be what the customer sees when they use their Amazon account to pay. You'll also want to enter a description of your application and link to your privacy notice. If you don't already have one, you'll need to find a generic one on the web and fill in the details to make it fit your store. You'll also have the opportunity to upload a logo, which will also be on the page that customers see when they are paying with Amazon.

You'll also need to do some configuration within the Amazon Payments site to make sure that Shopify is allowed to function as it was intended. Start with expanding the 'Web Settings' within the application and add the following URLs in the 'Javascript Origins section.

https://checkout.shopify.com
https://<yourstorename>.myshopify.com

You must also add the following URL in the 'Allowed Return URLs' section

https://checkout.shopify.com/<shop_id>/amazon_payments/callback

You'll also need to enter the Client ID from the application into your Shopify admin page.

For this last step, we're going to start at your Shopify admin page once again and click the gear icon to get back to settings. Then click Payments and go down to the Amazon Payments section. Click Activate once again and then you're going to connect your account, using the link provided. Enter your username and password and then use the check boxes to allow Shopify to access your Amazon account from your store. You'll also use the keys and numeric values you generated on Amazon to set values for Client ID, Seller ID and Authorization Token. As soon as you are done completely, Amazon Payments will become active within your Shopify admin page.

Alternative Payment Methods

There are over 70 alternative payment methods that Shopify can be configured with and which ones you have access to will depend entirely upon which country your Shopify store is located in. For example: if your store is within the United States, you'll be able to configure Dwolla, BitPay, CoinBase, GOcoin and Affirm.

Manual Payments

Of course, you can also set up your store to accept manual payments. By default, Shopify includes bank draft, COD and money orders, but if you prefer, there are other payment methods that you can set up within your manual payment settings.

Chapter Fourteen
Customizing Your Ecommerce Website

Before you actually launch your store, you'll want to customize it, not only so that all of the sections and widgets are in the right place, but also so that the design that you choose fits with the type of store that you have and is compatible and complementary to your color scheme, logos and other elements. In this chapter, we'll discuss the visual customization that can be done with Shopify and how to find the right template for your store, as well as how to use the design and task-based elements to give your site not just the perfect look, but the perfect layout as well, which will increase your chances of attracting customers.

The Purpose of this Chapter

This chapter was written with the goal of teaching you how to use the tools provided by Shopify to make your site look exactly the way that you want. While the customization tools that Shopify provides are extremely powerful, you might need to do some additional research on the themes that you encounter or on basic concepts like using complementary colors. In other words, this chapter is not intended to be the final word in Shopify design – rather it is intended to explain the basic concepts of customizing a Shopify website using themes and other accessories. If you want more advanced information you might have to do some more research.

The Shopify Help Manual

Shopify has a comprehensive help manual that you can use if you don't understand how a particular feature works of if you want to learn more about a function that there was enough space to go into in full detail here.

Shopify Themes

Shopify was created to function very similar to Wordpress and as such, many of the same names that you are familiar with from that platform will also be used here. For example, the way that you change the look of your store is through the use of a Shopify theme. Since you are paying for your Shopify site, the theme store has a large number of themes are that are completely free to use, but if you want to make your store look even better you can upgrade a premium theme. In order to access the theme store you can either click on the 'Online Store' link in your admin area sidebar and then choose themes, followed by 'Visit the Theme Store' or you can simply type in the URL on any browser window: themes.shopify.com.

Your Shopify Store Design

When you first set up your store, you're going to be doing a lot of work in the backend, like adding in your products, setting up shipping and all of the other tasks that are required in order for you to have a functional store. You won't have to worry too much about the look of your store until you are all done. However, eventually you want to take a look at the themes that are offered and decide which one fits the personality of your store the best. Here are some of the factors that will determine what your store design is going to look like.

The type of products that you're selling: Obviously, a store that is selling sports equipment will have a very different look from one selling intimate apparel or jewelry. You'll have to decide what sort of theme fits your products the best.
The personality of your store: This is a little different than the products that you are selling. Your store's personality may be based upon your own personality, or an idea that you have for your store to make it stylish and unique.
The budget for design: Obviously, if you have the type of budget that is going to force you to stick with the free Shopify themes you will be much more limited than someone who has money to spend on the theme.

There are four basic ways that you can use Shopify themes to make your site look amazing. Which one you choose will depend upon the factors detailed above. Let's start with free Shopify themes.

Free Themes from Shopify

When you sign up for Shopify, you get access to all of the free themes that they have available without any additional charge. The good news is, you don't have to search specifically for themes that are compatible with today's mobile devices because all of the themes provided by Shopify are responsive. Also, unlike Wordpress, these themes were designed with the specific purpose of selling things so you don't have to search for an ecommerce-friendly theme either. There are more than a hundred free themes from Shopify and nearly all of them are very high-quality themes that would make any store look great.

Shopify's Premium Themes

The second option you have for customizing your Shopify website is to use one of the premium themes that Shopify provides. These can also be found on the theme page. You just select premium and you'll get to choose between themes priced from $100 to $180 to customize your store with. Also, be aware that you can search both the free and the premium themes by industry including fashion, photography, electronics, sports and many more.

Shopify's Customization Options

Shopify has a large number of customization options when it comes to the themes that they have available, allowing you to tweak them any way you want, as long as you have the expertise to do so. Some of the customizations are very user-friendly and others require that you understand how the themes work, and some elements of graphic and website design in order to change certain aspects of a theme.

Custom Created Themes by Web Designers

There are a number of web designers out there who can create themes for Shopify, and if you already have a web designer that you like, Shopify provides instruction on how to create a theme that will work on their site. So, that's the fourth option that you have for getting your site to look the way that you want. You can create a custom design that you sketch out from scratch and have your web designer create it for you. This is often necessary in the case of stores that sell a particular product that just doesn't fit with any of the themes that are offered in the Shopify store. A web designer can create that perfect design that you envision your store having, and while this is the most expensive option, it might not be that much more than you would pay for a premium theme if you can find a designer willing to do it for a few hundred dollars.

Part Three:
Making your Shopify store a success

Chapter Seventeen
Other Features & Add-ons You Can Use With Shopify

You may not be aware that there are many other applications and software connections that you can integrate with your Shopify store. With all of the various programs that are being added each month, it is likely that even this list, current at the time of the writing, will be outdated by the time this book reaches you. But if you understand some of the programs that are now available, you will be able to find more of the same in the more recent programs offered, or simply newer versions of the ones mentioned here. At the very least, when you have completed this chapter you should be able to know where to look for add-on applications that will make it much easier to run your Shopify store.

Accounting: Accounting is one of the most important parts of your business management. You need to keep track of what you are spending and how much, so that you can make adjustments that will make your business as profitable as possible. In addition, you're going to need a down-to-the-penny tracking to report your taxes and have all of your paperwork in order if you need to defend your accounting in an audit. Luckily, Shopify can be integrated with some of the biggest third-party accounting software packages like Quickbooks, Freshbooks, Xero and more.

Inventory Management: You'll also need a way to keep track of your inventory and the tools that are offered by Shopify may not have every feature that you require. You can automate the process of replenishing inventory as little or as much as you'd like. You can track what the frequency of item sales so that you can get recommendations on which ones you need to replenish right away and which ones you can worry about later one because the chances are lower of them selling, and you can even automate the process of ordering if you like. Whatever inventory management setup you prefer, you can find a software solution that will provide it.

Customer Service: When it comes to customer service, you want to go the extra mile. You need people to feel as if they can get in touch with someone if they have a problem because otherwise, they might not buy from you in the future. There are a number of automated solutions that you can integrate into your Shopify store that will make your customer service better and easier to manage. From feedback and comment systems to live chat support, there are many ways that you can integrate third-part applications to make your customer service great.

Social Media Management: Social media management isn't just a good idea in today's online business, it is absolutely vital to the success of every ecommerce website out there. Social media management is definitely one of the aspects of your site that has the most automated tools associated with it. Whatever social media platforms that you are using, there is probably an application compatible with your Shopify store, and for the major ones, there are many. Shopify already has some integrated Facebook and Twitter tools available.

Marketing: Marketing is something else that you might need some extra help with. Because marketing is important no matter what kind of business you are in, but difficult to manage if you are a one-person ecommerce website, automated tools that help you market your products are definitely a plus. Often, marketing is combined with social media, but there may be other avenues that you're pursuing as well.

Sales: If you want to create more sales, you need to implement some compatible third-party programs that concentrate on things like upselling a customer, or giving them impulse buying options, as well as things like customer loyalty programs that make them want to come back.

Reporting: There are definitely some reporting tools that are already integrated into your Shopify store, but if you want to get more information than what these standard tools provide you might have to install third-party applications that give you more comprehensive reports. Things like what your customers viewed before they made a purchase, how long they spent on the purchase page, which products they skipped over and most definitely where they came from to get to your site are all details that you can gather and analyze to make your sales numbers higher.

Shipping: Shopify probably has one of the best shipping programs already integrated into the store. The way it works is this: a customer purchases an item from you, including the shipping cost. You then purchase the postage-included shipping label from Shopify at a discount – with the amount of the discount depending upon which plan you are currently enrolled in – and send your customer's item on its way. However, if you don't want to use the integrated shipping tools for whatever reason, Shopify does allow you to set up your own custom shipping options.

Misc. Tools: There are far too many tools out there that can be integrated into Shopify to include a list here, but what might help you further are some suggestions on where you can find these programs. One of the richest resources is right on Shopify's own user forum. There are probably hundreds of threads with programs that can be integrated into Shopify, and if you have a particular question, there are other Shopify users there, some of them with many years of experience, that can help.

Chapter Eighteen
Using Shopify's Learning Tools

One of the greatest tools that Shopify offers is something that you may not necessarily consider part of the value package that you get when you sign up for this store, but it is something that you would definitely miss if it were not included. Of course, we're discussing the Shopify help tools that come with the program. Because Shopify is so comprehensive and because there are so many third-party applications that can be integrated natively into Shopify, there is no way that all of the information needed to run a Shopify store could be included in a book – even a book this size. Luckily, Shopify has one of the best help sections of any ecommerce platform out there.

Accessing Shopify's Help System

Let's talk about how you navigate to Shopify's help system and how you get around there once you are in. If you are in your Shopify admin area, it is very difficult to navigate to the help section unless you stumble upon a link that takes you to a specific area. What makes that even more confusing is that there are several different help areas that you will encounter and you might be directed to a different URL. Here are the major help areas that Shopify provides.

https://ecommerce.shopify.com/
This is what is known as 'Ecommerce University' and it is a comprehensive help section that will take you through all of the different things that you'll need to know to become a successful ecommerce store owner. This isn't the same area as the main Shopify help area, although it does encompass some of the same or related information. What makes this area quite unique and very useful is that it actually gives you information and advice in making your store better and increasing your income in ways that will help you no matter if you are using the Shopify platform or not.

Shopify's Ecommerce University is divided up into four distinct sections.

Guides: The Guides are the first thing that you'll encounter on Shopify's Ecommerce University. The guides are comprehensive step-by-step instructions that will advise you on a number of topics from making your first sale to using dropshipping services. You can also find the guides at www.shopify.com/guides.

Blog: The blog is pretty standard but still extremely informative and has the advantage of featuring the latest information possible because it is updated regularly. On average, Shopify creates around four blog posts per week and the topics are all over the board, from using your Shopify platform better to some of the ecommerce topics that you'll want to learn to run a successful store like integrating with social media or starting your own blog to rank for keywords. The alternative URL for the blog is https://www.shopify.com/blog.

Forums: The forums are one of your most useful resources because you will be able to communicate directly with other Shopify users and this can help you solve problems, improve your store or educate yourself on ecommerce. The forums do not seem that large at first glance, with only about two dozen discussion boards but in fact, there are thousands of threads that you can browse and of course, the real strength of the forum is that you can create your own discussions and ask for advice specific to the problems you are having or even ask people to look at your store and give you suggestions for improvement. You can either access the forums from the link at Ecommerce University or you can go to https://ecommerce.shopify.com/forums.

Stories: One of the best places to visit before you even start setting up your store or make a commitment to join Shopify is the success stories page. This will not only give you motivation to start your own store, it will also give you ideas on how to make your store better or to find a niche that no one else is currently filling and become successful at it like the people in these success stories. Of course, for every success there are probably a thousand failures but it all comes down to how hard a person is willing to work. The link to this page is available from Ecommerce University or is located at: https://www.shopify.com/success-stories.

Shopify Documentation: The next help section that we'll cover is the documentation for the Shopify platform; there are four basic areas that are covered by the documentation: Using Shopify Online, Using Shopify POS (Point-of-Sale), Designing Shopify Apps and Designing Shopify Themes. Two of them are useful for store owners and the other two are intended for those designing programs or themes to work with Shopify. You can use the search function to search within these topics and find documentation on these particular topics. The documentation page is located at https://docs.shopify.com/.

Shopify Manual: The last part of the documentation is the most important part for store owners. It is a comprehensive guide on how to use Shopify, from top to bottom, with screenshots and animations to explain how to do just about everything, including how to set up Shopify features on Amazon and Paypal. The section of the documentation called "Using Shopify Online" pulls almost exclusively from the manual and there are several sections within that topic that are broken down by the manual. They include: orders, discounts, customers, collections, reports, gift cards and more. You can access the manual by going to https://docs.shopify.com/manual.

Chapter Nineteen
Niche Marketing

There are many different types of products that you can sell in your Shopify store. While there have been people that have made a success with a very general product niche such as 'sporting goods' the majority of people cannot compete in a market saturated by big name brick-and-mortar companies that have been years (and millions of dollars) building their online presence. Most notably, Amazon is a company that pretty much blows everyone else out of the water on everything from electronics to clothing to just about every odd and end that you can imagine. Luckily, Amazon is so big that they are unable to offer one thing: niche expertise. That's where your most viable marketing chances are.

What is Niche Marketing?

Niche marketing is the purposeful design of a website, company or organization dedicated to a product that a very small portion of the population desires. Items that are not niche items are those that are used by just about everyone. For example: shoes. Everyone in developed countries (and in most undeveloped countries as well) buys shoes and many of them buy them online. But there are so many shoe companies – many of them large corporations with huge online marketing budgets – that it would be almost impossible to compete in that particular field.

Niche marketing, on the other hand, is effective because there are very few people – and ideally almost no one – serving that particular need. For example, Tom's Shoes could be thought of a niche marketing venture. When you buy a pair of Tom's Shoes the company donates a pair of shoes to a child in need. This niche that was created was a charitable donation along with a pair of shoes. You could feel good about spending money there.

Of course, there are much more common types of niche marketing as well. For example, ballet slippers are much more refined niche items within the shoe industry. This is a well-balanced niche where there isn't nearly as much competition (although still quite a bit) but also something that is in demand. An unsuccessful niche is one that is not being served by anyone but where the market is so small as to be unprofitable.

How to Find a Niche

If you want to do niche marketing successfully the first thing that you're going to have to do is find a niche. The easiest way to find a niche that you will be able to compete it is not through market research or suggestions online, but rather, to find something that you are passionate about and then find a way to sell products or services related to that online. Someone who is dedicated to extreme sports might enjoy running a store that sells extreme sports equipment, books on extreme sports and other such products.

There is a definite benefit to finding a niche this way. One of the reasons that people choose to go with a niche website for the products they need rather than a big retailer that might save them money is that they desire the expertise that a niche website offers. For example: a retailer like Walmart or Amazon might not base their product inventory on what items are the top of the line or recommended by experts when it comes to a category like extreme sports, but a niche website run by someone who is an expert in the field probably will.

How to Market a Niche Website

There are several ways that you can market your niche website. The first is by choosing a niche that you can represent as an expert. That doesn't mean that you necessarily have to be a complete expert in the niche when you begin, but it should start with you having a passion for the topic. You can learn what you need to know from that point and continue to improve your expertise over time.

The second thing that you'll want to do to market your niche store is to begin to build a reputation for expertise. This means that you'll need to publish content that can be attributed to you or your Shopify niche store that is considered expert advice within your field. Most of the time, this is done by creating a blog. Luckily, Shopify already includes the ability to create a blog right in your store's admin area – probably because they see the value that having a blog brings to an ecommerce niche website.

Your blog posts should consist of expert advice about your niche that you know people will be searching for. Once you have established your expertise, it will be easier to get people to visit your store from the blog, and it will be easier to get those people to come back in the future. However, you still should do solid keyword research and maintain best SEO practices to get as much traffic as possible.

Another way that you can establish your expertise and drive traffic to your website is by answering questions or commenting on a forum related to your niche. Obviously, you want to make sure that you are allowed to put a link to your store in your signature or else you might not get very much benefit from all of the posting that you are doing on that forum. If you put your store name and link in your signature and you provide valuable content and advice within the forum, you are definitely going to drive traffic to your site, and those links will probably continue to drive traffic as long as the forum is active.

Of course, all of this is a lot of work if you have limited time. Writing blog posts is something that you can easily outsource as you don't necessarily need to find someone who is an expert in your niche – just a quality freelance writer who will put in the time and do the research. As for forum posting, you probably want to do this yourself. You are building up a personality for yourself and your store and you want this personality to reflect you correctly.

Quick Checklist to Choosing a Niche Topic

Here are some questions that you can ask yourself to determine whether or not a niche topic is viable.

Is the price high enough to make decent money even on low sales volume?
Are people making money in this niche?
Is the competition professional or are they small, ecommerce sites like yours?
Could you write 100 articles on the topic (or do the research to write 100 articles)?

Chapter Twenty
Using Social Media Effectively

One of the things that you're going to have to do if you want your store to succeed is use social media to promote your business and communicate with your customers. These days, a business without a social media connection is as dead-in-the-water as a company in the 1970's or 1980's would have been without a telephone. Social media is just one of the earmarks of a professional company and it is one of the best ways to advertise, offer customer support and let customers know that there are real people behind your organization.

The Basics of Social Media

You know that social media can be a great way to get traffic to your ecommerce website but that doesn't mean that getting that traffic is going to be easy. It especially is going to take work if you want to have sustained success throughout your store's lifetime. That means that you aren't just looking for short-term social media tactics, you actually need a strategy. That begins with goal-setting.

Setting goals is important no matter what you are trying to achieve, because unless you know where you are going you have very little chance of getting there. You want to set goals like: traffic increases from social media, number of followers/fans/other vernacular of your social media platform, your conversion rate, post engagement numbers and growth goals.

You also need to know what your customers need. This was discussed a little bit in the chapter on niche marketing. You definitely want to know what kind of content they desire before you start posting and then monitor and stay in the loop using social media, comments and other methods to track reactions. The analytics that come with your website also can provide you with a great deal of information on what your customers are looking for and what kind of posts would bring in the most traffic. The keywords that people use when they reach your site are particularly telling and can be an unlimited source of topics to write about.

Finally, one of the most basic things about social media that anyone just coming in should understand is that social media isn't for selling. While you can make sales using social media, and it can be a great selling tool, your primary purpose should be sharing with your followers or fans. If you try to make your social media platform a podium from which to hawk your products, you are going to lose your followers very quickly.

However, if you can keep followers interested in your feed – whatever platform you are using – you will find that new followers will always come and your regular followers will not be offended by the occasional product recommendation from your store, particularly if it is something that solves a problem that someone was introducing on social media. Just remember to keep track of your progress and that your social media efforts are showing improvement.

Ten Social Media Strategies for Ecommerce

Here are some social media strategies that have been shown to be particularly effective in ecommerce. These are definitely things that you should strive for, but if you aren't performing up to 100% on everything (or anything for that matter) don't worry – because as long as you are improving – your income from social media will be improving as well.

1. Make sure you are thinking carefully about what words you use in your social media posts. You don't want to write just anything. For one thing, it is going to live on the internet forever, so if you are giving advice, triple-check to make sure it is accurate. However, what is probably more important is that you use keyword research when you create social media posts. You'll be able to get your social media posts higher in search and as a result, attract more followers.

2. Share images whenever possible. Your followers and anyone else who views your posts are going to be scanning the web like everyone does and you need to be able to grab their attention and get them to actually read your content.

3. Sharing your reviews can be one of the most effective sales tools that you have. When someone leaves a positive review share it on social media and then sit back and watch the sales roll in. People trust online reviews almost as much as they do the recommendation of a trusted friend.

4. Make it easy for someone to share your content with others. Make sure that you are following a strategy and creating buttons that are in a location most likely to be used by your readers. The easier that you make it for people to share your content the more likely it is that they will. If you find something that is working, stick with it and be consistent so that people know where to look for it.

5. You are on social media to create a human face behind your business so make sure that you actually interact with your followers. Read their posts, and comment on them when appropriate and do everything that you would do for a friend that you are following on a personal social media account. Of course, the more followers you have the more limited your personal interactions have to be, but the point is to make sure that your followers know that you actually care about them and don't just see them as dollar signs.

6. Join any groups that are related to your niche or industry. If your social media platform offers groups, make sure you join them, and use this the same way that you would a forum related to your chosen topic – post great content that will be viewed as "expert" content.

7. Find out who the influencers are in your niche and build relationships with those people. Every niche has people that have a lot of weight behind them on certain topics. Obviously, the ideal situation would be for you to be that influencer, but even if that is the case, building relationships with other influencers can do nothing but help you.

8. Post consistently. This is probably the number one touted social media tip on the web and for good reason. People that post consistently get the most followers, the most interaction from the followers that they have and they build the best brand

image. If you don't have time for this, consider outsourcing or using social media automation tools to provide consistency.

9. Use hashtags but don't be ridiculous. You don't need to create a hashtag with every single post that you make and you definitely don't want to use multiple "cute" hashtags on every post but if you can use hashtags that don't make people want to unfollow you you'll get a big boost in traffic from the people searching for those hashtags.

10. Brevity is the key to interaction. If you want people to check out your content create engaging post titles and make your posts as short and concise as possible. While you should definitely make your blog posts and advice comprehensive enough to provide valuable information, always be thinking of ways that you can shorten things to create more engagement.

Chapter Twenty-One
Spotting & Cashing in on Trends

One of the ways that you can improve your earnings from your website, and potentially gain a lot of social media followers and future buyers, is to get in on trends that are just starting. This is a very viable strategy, even for the smallest ecommerce website, because if you can get your post in front of all of the other people jumping on a trend, your traffic could be at the level of a viral post or video. You could go from a steady 10,000 visits per month to millions of visitors in just one day, just by jumping on a current trend and most importantly – recognizing it will become a trend before anyone else does.

How to Spot a Trend

So, how do you spot a trend? Unfortunately, this has no easy answer. If it did, just about everyone would be able to capitalize on trends and make money from them, and it would only be the biggest companies that were getting in front of trends. This is one area where a smaller website really can succeed because recognizing a trend has a lot more to do with luck than with skill. While there isn't a way that you can train yourself to spot trends there are some best practices for putting yourself in a position to spot them, and the more practice you have at seeing coming trends the easier it will become.

The first thing that you need to be aware of is that trends are found just about everywhere and that you should look out for them whenever you are watching television, browsing the web or even listening to music. Successful writers have to cultivate the sense of recognizing ideas (especially good ideas) when they come along and this is the same sort of sense that a trend-watcher should try to create. You want to recognize a potential trend when it comes along and develop skills and experience to know when that trend is worth pursuing. Here are some tips that will help you do exactly that.

Know Your Buyers

The shopping habits of baby boomers have long been the shopping demographic that companies have set their marketing budget by. But baby boomers are no longer the buying power that they once were. In fact, it is the directly subsequent generations that have the majority of buying power these days and in order to recognize trends you need to know what appeals to them. Today's shoppers (and it is likely you are one of them) have specific attributes and trends that appeal to them might be different than what the biggest companies are predicting. That's why it took large corporations a great deal of time to understand viral videos and why some companies are still struggling.

Know What Has Worked in the Past

If you want to know what possible future trends are going to be you need to know what has worked in the past. Study past trends and be familiar with why they become trendy and pay attention to factors like the longevity of the trend, the overall popularity and any external factors that might have affected that particular trend becoming popular. There are a number of companies that track past trends and there is a lot of information online that can help you with your research.

Pay Attention to Regular Trends

Google has a tool that specifically allows you to search for trends for a particular topic, and one thing that you should be looking for in your particular niche is times of the year when your topic peaks or flatlines. These are part of the trends that you should be paying attention to when you have an e-store because it can help you decide when to step up your marketing efforts or take advantage of sales booms.

Know the Right Websites

There are websites out there that are specifically devoted to trends. Buzzfeed is one of the most well-known ones but there are many others as well. If you can find some of them that you can get updates from or check out once in a while you might get a leg up on some trends. Mashable is another well-known site that follows trends. Another great technique is to use Google and type in predictions and see what experts are predicting for your particular niche.

Chapter Twenty-Two
Holiday Selling

If you have an online store, one of the things that you're going to look forward to every year (more than usual even) is the holiday season. Holiday sales are always higher than other times of the year, for nearly every niche out there, and some companies even make the majority of their revenue for the entire year during the holiday season. You can take advantage of this shopping boom if you are prepared and set to go, and luckily, the fact that you have a Shopify store allows you to get ahead of much of the competition.

How Much of a Sales Boost Can You Expect?

Ecommerce holiday sales are going to be bigger than ever and that is going to be the case for some time to come. Traditionally, people spent most of their holiday money in brick-and-mortar stores but as people become busier and it becomes easier to order online – particularly with the huge boom of mobile ordering – the ecommerce route is going to be the way that nearly everyone goes in coming years and retailers are switching their holiday focus to online shopping. It will depend upon your particular niche how much of a boost you will see over your regular sales, as well as your marketing efforts and products that you are listing, but if you have an ecommerce website you are poised to be there when holiday shoppers go searching for gifts.

Tips on Making the Most of Your Holiday Season

There are definitely some ways that you can improve your chances of having a successful and rewarding holiday season with your e-store. Here are some tips to help you make the most of the upcoming holiday shopping boom.

Mobile Shopping

One of the major advantages that Shopify gives you is that you have a responsive website and checkout that will work on any mobile device. That's good, because in 2015 holiday shopping on mobile devices increased by nearly 50%. The projections for upcoming years say that if your website isn't responsive and your checkout process isn't mobile-friendly, you aren't going to be able to compete with other ecommerce websites when the holidays roll around.

Preparing Early

The second tip that you'll want to follow is to get started early. This doesn't mean starting in November, or even October. You want to actually prepare for the upcoming holiday season six months in advance. That includes ensuring that your mobile checkout works properly, that you know what sort of marketing methods you are going to be using to advertise for the holidays and that you have everything in place for the season when it gets here.

Part of that is because there are probably going to be twice as many things to do to prepare – particularly if this is your first holiday season – than you expect there to be and the other reason is that people tend to start their shopping early. By the beginning of November, you should be launching your holiday campaigns, not just getting started on them. If you start in November, you are going to miss the holiday shopping season altogether.

Change Website Copy

The holidays are the time to spruce up bland website copy and even change much of it to reflect the shopping season. The benefit of this is that you'll get a boost for having new content which means more search traffic and in addition, you'll be able to insert holiday keywords that you know people are searching for.

With Shopify, you can import your products from a format like a CSV file. The benefit of doing this is that you can change certain elements, such as the description of a product or group of products and then save it for later. For example, some people have several sets of product descriptions for the same products that they import depending upon the season. With holiday shopping this is a great way to optimize your site for the hordes of ecommerce shoppers. If you don't have a CSV with your product information on it, you can export your list of products to a file like this and then change the descriptions and import the new descriptions all at once.

Point out Gifts

Another great use of the visual elements and text is to remind people that certain items make great gifts. Of course, this can work at any time of the year, as people look for wedding gifts, birthday gifts and more all throughout the year, but it is most effective during the holiday season. If you can choose certain products that you think would make great gifts and then add a graphic or line of text somewhere in the description that reminds people of how great of a gift the product would make you will see an increase in your sales during the holiday season.

Use Your Social Media Power to Remind Shoppers

Another way that you can increase sales is by using your social media platforms to remind people that they need to buy a gift. The trick here is to appear subtle while making sure that they get the message. One way to do this is by discussing the upcoming holiday season on social media or create lists of gift ideas on your blog. You don't have to beat your followers over the head with the fact that you have a store selling great holiday gift items, but you do want to make sure that they remember once in a while so that you have a chance of converting them.

Decorate for the Holidays

Consider changing your theme or doing some customization for the holiday season. That way, when people visit your store they are reminded of the gifts that they need to purchase in the near future and will be apt to look at some of the gift ideas that you have to offer, even if they had originally come to your store for non-holiday shopping.

Conclusion

Whether you are brand new to the ecommerce business or you are an experienced seller online, Shopify can certainly help you make more money, create more effective ecommerce stores and overall, be a better online seller. Let's review some of the things discussed in this book.

Part One: Introduction to Ecommerce

If you have never been involved in the world of ecommerce before, it can be a challenging one to start. Ecommerce depends upon getting customers to your website and it is quite a bit different than starting a brick-and-mortar business. In fact, you could take the analogy so far as to say that starting an ecommerce business is like starting a little store that looks like every other store in a city that has hundreds of millions of stores. While you can rent a retail space on the main drag and get lots of walk-in traffic in the real world the only way that you are going to get to the front page in the search engines is through the use of good SEO practices, keyword research and understanding the business of ecommerce completely.

That's why part one starts out with showing you what you need to know to be involved in this world. Product selection is one of the most important things that you can do because your product name is often what people search for and if you can choose the right products that are going to outrank other websites selling the same items; you are going to get the majority of the customers. In addition, understanding things like the market size of your niche, the customer that you are trying to appeal to and who else on the web is competing with you for those customers are all factors that will determine how successful you're going to be.

When you begin working with Shopify, you are going to quickly realize that there is a lot to learn about ecommerce and while you don't need to know everything to get started, the more quickly you can learn things like making yourself unique among your competition, as discussed in Chapter 5, the faster you will be successful. Understanding your product types, the laws regarding your ecommerce business and all of the other information that you need to be successful are things that you should be teaching yourself as quickly as possible. Don't be afraid to learn from online videos, lectures, seminars and even classes offered in your community.

Part Two: Setting up Shopify

Learning the business of ecommerce is definitely important, but if you are going to be using the Shopify platform it is just as important that you understand Shopify and learn everything you can about how to use it. The reason is: Shopify is an incredibly powerful application and if you don't learn everything you can about how to use it properly you are going to be missing out on sales. You will probably be successful even if you only learn some of what the platform has to offer, but why would you want to limit your ability to make money.

Some of the ways that you can learn how to use Shopify better is included in this book, but there is a great deal more information that is provided by the Shopify platform itself, using the help guides, the manual, documentation and the other Shopify resources that are listed in Chapter 18.

In the second part of this book, we've discussed how to choose the right Shopify package and what all of the various features mean for your business. Also, you have probably come to the conclusion that the Shopify platform is a great deal more powerful than just about anything else out there and should definitely be your top choice if you want to be a successful ecommerce business owner.

Part Two has included the five basic steps that you need to get your store up and running which are as follows:

- Your initial setup – all of the things that you'll do to get your store started with Shopify and be prepared to add your first products.

- Adding your products – something that has a great deal of customization behind it and something that you definitely should learn all about using the materials in the Shopify manual before you even add your first product.

- Setting up your shipping – this is a fairly straightforward process, although it is quite powerful in its own right, and Shopify makes it easier than most. In fact, Shopify not only makes it easier on their customers than most, they make it more cost-effective as well, which is good for your bottom line every time you sell something.

- Customizing your payment solutions – You have a lot of integrated payment solutions when it comes to Shopify and there are some powerful options. But perhaps the biggest advantage that the platform has over all of the others out there is that it provides you with such a simple payment solution with low fees and no need to set up third-party merchant accounts. If you don't want to, you don't need to go any farther than Shopify Payments to get paid for your sales.

- Customizing your Shopify store – Shopify makes it easy to create the perfect look for your store with over 100 free themes that all look very professional and even more premium themes for those who are a bit pickier.

Part Three: Making Your Shopify Store a Success

The last part of the book deals with applications and details outside of the Shopify platform that you can use to make your store even better. The features and add-ons that can be integrated with Shopify are numerous and should definitely be evaluated to see if they would make your store better.

One of the most important chapters of this section is Chapter 18, where you will be able to see all of the learning tools that Shopify provides. From the documentation and comprehensive manual complete with screenshots and animations, to the user forums where you can get specific advice on problems that you are facing directly from other Shopify users. In addition, this chapter expands on some of the more important aspects of ecommerce such as using social media to make your store more effective and making more money through the use of trends and holiday shopping.

Your Success is up to you

When it comes to the success of your store, there is only one person that it depends upon – you. While you have a huge number of tools and resources available to you with the Shopify platform and all of the benefits that comes with it, none of that will make much of a difference if you aren't willing to put in the work to make your store a success. However, even for the most uninformed ecommerce owner, success can be had with Shopify if you choose good products and follow the advice in this book and from experts in the field of ecommerce and continue learning and improving as you make money.

Printed in the USA
CPSIA information can be obtained
at www.ICGtesting.com
LVHW050104290724
786756LV00030B/681

9 781523 863938